STUDY NOTES

CURRENT AFFAIRS January 2023

CONTENT TABLE

CURRENT AFFAIRS JANUARY 2023

TOPICS	PAGE NO
17th Pravasi Bhartiya Samman Award 2023 Announced	04 - 06
17th Pravasi Bhartiya Divas 2023	07 - 08
Mascot, Torch, and Anthem of Khelo India Youth Games 2022	08 - 08
World Hindi Day 2023	09 - 10
Golden Globes Winners 2023 Announced	10 - 11
Henley Passport Index 2023, Japan Retained Its Top Position	11 - 13
Nation celebrates National Youth Day on January 12	13 - 14
Miss Universe 2022	14 - 14
Critics' Choice Awards 2023	15 - 16
Amazon back as World's Most Valued Brand, Apple down to No 2	16 - 17
Brand Guardianship Index 2023	17 - 19
Parakram Diwas 2023	19 - 19
ICC Men's and Women's T20I Team of The Year 2022	19 - 19
Padma Awards 2023 Winners	19 - 27
Republic Day 2023	27 - 30
ICC annual awards 2022	30 - 30

Gallantry Awards	30 - 32
Australian Open 2023	33 - 34
Banking and Financial Current Affairs	34 - 38
Economy Current Affairs	38 - 41
Business Current Affairs	41 - 44
International Current Affairs	44 - 51
National Current Affairs	51 - 58
States Current Affairs	58 - 64
Schemes/Committees News	64 - 66
Agreement/Memorandum of Understanding (MoU)	66 - 69
Ranks and Reports	69 - 72
Sports Current Affairs	72 - 77
Summits and conferences	77 - 79
Awards & Recognition	79 - 82
Important Days	82 - 86
Defence Current Affairs	86 - 91
Science and Technology	91 - 95
Books & Authors	95 - 97
Miscellaneous Current Affairs	97 - 102
Obituaries	102 - 105

JANUARY 2023 CURRENT AFFAIRS

17th Pravasi Bharatiya Samman Award 2023 Announced

17th Pravasi Bharatiya Samman Award

27 Indians living overseas have been chosen by the Indian government for the Pravasi Bharatiya Samman Awards (PBSA), for outstanding achievements both in India and abroad. The award is the highest honour conferred upon Indians living abroad, including Non-Resident Indians (NRIs), Persons of Indian Origin (PIOs) or organisations/institutions established and run by them.

The jury that selected the recipients comprised VicePresident Jagdeep Dhankhar as its chairman and External Affairs Minister S Jaishankar as its Vice-Chair, among other distinguished dignitaries from different fields. The awards will be conferred upon the recipients by President Droupadi Murmu during the 17th edition of the PBSA, which is scheduled to be held from 8-10 January in Indore, Madhya Pradesh.

Theme of 17th Pravasi Bharatiya Samman Award

As per the Ministry of External Affairs, the theme for Pravasi Bharatiya Divas 2023 will be "Diaspora: Reliable Partners for India's Progress in Amrit Kaal". This theme highlights the importance of the Indian diaspora in contributing to India's progress.

List of Overseas Indians Chosen for the Honour

S.no	Person	Country	Field
1	Jagadish Chennupati	Australia	Science & Technology/ Education
2	Sanjeev Mehta	Bhutan	Education
3	Dilip Loundo	Brazil	Art & Culture/Education
4	Alexander Maliakel John	Brunei Darussalam	Medicine
5	Vaikuntam Iyer Lakshmanan	Canada	Community Welfare

6	Joginder Singh Nijjar	Croatia	Art & Culture/Educa-tion
7	Ramjee Prasad	Denmark	Information Technology
8	Kannan Ambalam	Ethiopia	Community Welfare
9	Amal Kumar Mukho-padhyay	Community Wel-fare/Medicine	Germany
10	Mohamed Irfaan Ali (Guyana President)	Guyana	Politics/Community Welfare
11	Reena Vinod Pushkarna	Israel	Business/Community Welfare
12	Maqsood Sarfi Shiotani	Japan	Education
13	Rajagopal	Mexico	Education
14	Amit Kailash Chandra Lath	Poland	Business/Community Welfare
15	Parmanand Sukhumal Daswani	Republic of Congo	Community Welfare
16	Piyush Gupta	Singapore	Business
17	Mohanlal Hira	South Africa	Community Welfare
18	Sanjaykumar Shivabhai Patel	South Sudan	Business/Community Welfare
19	Sivakumar Nadesan	Sri Lanka	Community Welfare
20	Dewanchandrebhose Sharman	Suriname	Community Welfare
21	Archana Sharma	Switzerland	Science & Technology
22	Frank Arthur Seepersad	Trinidad & Tobago	Community Wel-fare/Education

23	Siddharth Balachandran	UAE	Business/Community Welfare
24	Chandrakant Babubhai Patel	UK	Media
25	Darshan Singh Dhaliwal	USA	Business/Community Welfare
26	Rajesh Subramaniam	USA	Business
27	Ashok Kumar Tiwary	Uzbekistan	Business

About the Pravasi Bharatiya Samman

The Pravasi Bharatiya Samman (Overseas Indian Honour/Award) is the highest Indian award for Nonresident Indian and Overseas Citizen of India or an organisation or institution established and run by NonResident Indians or Persons of Indian Origin, constituted by the Ministry of Overseas Indian Affairs, Government of India in conjunction with the Pravasi Bharatiya Divas (NonResident Indian Day), to honour exceptional and meritorious contribution in their chosen field/profession. The award is given by the President of India. Since 2016, the Government of India has doubled the number of awardees each year to 30 after a decision to grant the award once every two years.

Pravasi Bharatiya Samman (PBS) is conferred for outstanding contributions in any of the following areas:

- "Social and humanitarian causes in India or abroad"
- "Better understanding of India"
- "Support to India's causes and concerns in a tangible way" - "Building closer links between India, the overseas Indian community and their country of residence;"
- "Welfare of the local Indian community"
- "Philanthropic and charitable work"
- "Eminence in one's field or outstanding work, which has enhanced India's prestige in the country of residence; or"
- "Eminence in skills which has enhanced India's prestige in that country (for non-professional workers)."

17th Pravasi Bhartiya Divas 2023

Pravasi Bharatiya Divas or NRI Day is formally observed on 9 January to celebrate the day when Mahatma Gandhi returned from South Africa to Mumbai, India. The day is celebrated to acknowledge the contribution of the nonresident Indian community in helping in the development of the country. Pravasi Bharatiya Divas 2023 has conducted in Indore, Madhya Pradesh, from 8-10 January, 2023. It is important to note that this is the 17th Pravasi Bharatiya Divas, or NRI Day.

Pravasi Bharatiya Divas 2023: Theme

According to the Ministry of External Affairs, the official theme of the Pravasi Bharatiya Divas 2023 is "Diaspora: Reliable Partners for India's Progress in Amrit Kaal." The theme focuses on the importance of the Indian diaspora in the development of the country. It is important to note that every year a new theme is chosen to celebrate the day.

Pravasi Bharatiya Divas 2023: Significance

The purpose of Pravasi Bharatiya Divas is to give NRIs a forum to discuss their attitudes toward India and to build bridges of goodwill with their fellow citizens. It also entails informing the natives of their brothers' accomplishments abroad and informing the foreigners of what their fellow citizens expect of them.

Another goal of the organisation is to establish a network of Indians living abroad in 110 different nations. educating the general public on the contribution that immigrants have made to India's positive international relations. establishing a link between the rising Indian generation and the immigrant brethren. to talk about the challenges that Indian workers encounter when working abroad.

Pravasi Bharatiya Divas: History

The decision to celebrate Pravasi Bharatiya Divas was taken in accordance with recommendations of the High Level Committee (HLC) on the Indian Diaspora set up by government of India under the chairmanship of L. M. Singhvi. The then Prime Minister of India, Shri Atal Bihari Vajpayee, received the report of the Committee at a public function at Vigyan Bhavan in New Delhi on 8 January 2002, and announced the "Pravasi Bharatiya Divas" (PBD) on 9 January 2002. The day was chosen to mark the return of Mahatma Gandhi from South Africa to India in 1915.

After this day was administered in 2000, it was first celebrated in 2003. Here are more insights concerning the historical backdrop of Pravasi Bharatiya Divas - The Pravasi Bhartiya Divas date is the 9th of January. Most people celebrated this as NRI Day in India. NRI Day and pravasi Bhartiya divas is the same thing.

Mascot, Torch and Anthem of Khelo India Youth Games 2022

Khelo India Youth Game 2022

The anthem, mascot and a 'smart torch' for the fifth edition of the youth games were unveiled by chief minister Shivraj Singh Chouhan, Union MoS sports Nisith Pramanik and state sports minister at a glittering event in Bhopal on Saturday evening. The highlight was a drone show that created magic in Bhopal's night sky with hundreds of drones forming a sprinting cheetah, maps of India and Madhya Pradesh and 'Khelo India Youth Games 2022' The Games will be organised in eight districts of Madhya Pradesh from January 30 , with Malkhamb and water sports making their debut.

The 5th KIYG 2022 will be held from January 30 to February 11. There are 27 sporting disciplines on the schedule, with over 6,000 athletes competing. 'Hindustan Ka Dil Dhadka Do' - this is the heartpounding anthem of the Khelo India Youth Games 2022. And cheetah Asha, who was named by PM Narendra Modi, the Games mascot.

About Khelo India

The importance of sports and fitness in one's life is invaluable. Playing sports inculcates team spirit, develops strategic & analytical thinking, leadership skills, goal setting and risk taking. A fit and healthy individual leads to an equally healthy society and strong nation.

Sports is an extremely important component for the overall development of our nation. India, in the last few years has made steady progress in the field of sports. This tremendous potential needs to be showcased at a global platform. It's time we inspire young talent, give them top-notch infrastructure and training of the highest level. We need to inculcate a strong spirit of participation in sports that enables players to demonstrate their true potential. Only then can India realise its dream of becoming a sports super power. The Khelo India programme has been introduced to revive the sports culture in India at the grass-root level by building a strong framework for all sports played in our country and establish India as a great sporting nation.

World Hindi Day 2023

World Hindi Day or Vishwa Hindi Diwas is celebrated on 10th January every year to promote awareness about the language across the world. It is also the day when Hindi, India's national language, was spoken for the first time in the United Nations General Assembly. It was on this day in 1975 that the first World Hindi Conference was held in Nagpur. Since then, such conferences are organised in different parts of the world every year.

Notably: The language got its name from the Persian term 'Hind' which means 'the land of Indus'. The language is spoken in India, Trinidad, Nepal, Guyana, Mauritius and other countries.

Theme of World Hindi Conference 2023

The theme this year is "Hindi - Traditional Knowledge to Artificial Intelligence". This year, the 12th World Hindi Conference will be organised in Fiji by the Foreign Ministry in collaboration with the Fiji government from February 15 to 17 . The location for the 2023 event was decided during the 11th World Hindi Conference held in Mauritius last year.

Significance of World Hindi Day 2023

The World Hindi Day or Vishwa Hindi Diwas is commemorated to mark the importance of Hindi as a language. It is considered one of the official national languages in India, especially in the northern part of the country. The day is also celebrated to represent the Hindispeaking community on a global level. On the occasion of World Hindi Day, the Ministry of External Affairs organises several events around the world to spread more knowledge about Hindi.

History of World Hindi Day

The Union of India adopted Hindi as its official language in 1950. According to Article 343, the Constitution of India states that the official language of India shall be Hindi in Devanagari script. The first World Hindi Conference was envisioned by Rashtrabhasha Prachar Samiti, Wardha in 1973. It was organized in Nagpur on January 10, 1975. Its aim was to promote the language on a global level. The conference saw the participation of 30 countries with 122 representatives.

Vishwa Hindi Diwas was first celebrated in 2006 under the instructions of then-Prime Minister Manmohan Singh. The date of January 10 was chosen as Hindi was spoken for the first time in the United Nations General Assembly on January 10, 1949 . In 1975, the World Hindi Conference was formed by then Prime Minister Indira Gandhi for bringing together Hindi scholars, writers and laureates who have contributed to the development of the language and appreciate their contributions.

Golden Globes Winners 2023 Announced

The 80th edition of 2023 Golden Globes show, hosted by Jerrod Carmichael, airs live on NBC and Peacock. The 80th Golden Globe Awards is the first edition of the annual spectacle to be on TV since an ethics, finance and diversity scandal involving the Hollywood Foreign Press Association, the group behind the awards, led NBC to decide not to air the 2022 ceremony. As in years past, the show will hand out honors in both film and TV categories.

Follow below for updates as winners are announced

Category	Winners
Best TV Series, Musical or Comedy	"Abbott Elementary"
Best Performance by an Actor in a TV Series, Drama	Kevin Costner, "Yellowstone"
Best Director, Motion Picture	Steven Spielberg, "The Fabelmans"
Best Screenplay, Motion Picture	Martin McDonagh, "The Banshees of Inisherin"
Best Motion Picture, Non-English Language	"Argentina, 1985"
Best Performance by an Actress in a Motion Picture, Drama	Cate Blanchett, "Tár"
Best Performance by an Actress in a TV Series, Drama	Zendaya, "Euphoria"
Best Performance by an Actor in a Motion Picture, Drama	Austin Butler, "Elvis"

Best Motion Picture, Animated	"Guillermo del Toro's Pinocchio"
Best Performance by an Actress in a Motion Picture, Musical or Comedy	Michelle Yeoh, "Everything Everywhere All at Once"
Best Performance by an Actor in a Motion Picture, Musical or Comedy	Colin Farrell, "The Banshees of Inisherin"
Best Performance by an Actress in a TV Series, Musical or Comedy	Quinta Brunson, "Abbott Elementary"
Best Performance by an Actor in a TV Series, Musical or Comedy	Jeremy Allen White, "The Bear"
Best Original Song, Motion Picture	"Naatu Naatu," "RRR"
Best Original Score, Motion Picture	Justin Hurwitz, "Babylon"

Henley Passport Index 2023, Japan Retained Its Top Position

According to the latest Henley Passport Index, Japan has retained its position as the most favourible passport in the world, allowing visa-free entry to 193 global destinations. which the country tops for the fifth consecutive year. Singapore and South Korea came in a joint second on the ranking, followed by Germany and Spain, and then a slew of other European nations.

Where does India rank?

The Indian passport was ranked 85th, giving visa-free entry to 59 destinations worldwide. In 2019, 2020, 2021 and 2022, the country ranked at 82nd spot, 84th, 85th and 83rd respectively. Indian passport holders can travel visa-free to 59 destinations like Bhutan, Indonesia, Macao, Maldives, Nepal, Sri Lanka, Thailand, Kenya, Mauritius, Seychelles, Zimbabwe, Uganda, Iran and Qatar. However, some countries require visa-on-arrival.

India's Neighbouring country

- China (80 destinations)
- Sri Lanka (42 destinations)

- Bangladesh (41 destinations)
- Nepal (38 destinations)
- Pakistan (32 destinations)

Here's the list of the top 10 strongest passports in the world

- Japan (193 destinations)
- Singapore, South Korea (192 destinations)
- Germany, Spain (190 destinations)
- Finland, Italy, Luxembourg (189 destinations)
- Austria, Denmark, Netherlands, Sweden (188 destinations)
- France, Ireland, Portugal, United Kingdom (187 destinations)
- Belgium, New Zealand, Norway, Switzerland, United, States, Czech Republic (186 destinations)
- Australia, Canada, Greece, Malta (185 destinations)
- Hungary, Poland (184 destinations)
- Lithuania, Slovakia (183 destinations)

List of 10 countries that fall in the bottom 10

- Sri Lanka/Sudan (42)
- Bangladesh/Kosovo/Libya (41)
- North Korea (40 destinations)
- Nepal, Palestinian territory (38 destinations)
- Somalia (35 destinations)
- Yemen (34 destinations)
- Pakistan (32 destinations)
- Syria (30 destinations)
- Iraq (29 destinations)
- Afghanistan (27 destinations)

About the Henley Passport Index

The ranking, published by London-based immigration consultancy Henley & Partners, uses data from the International Air Transport Association to rank 199 passports' access to 227 travel destinations. The methodology differs from other passport indexes like one published by financial advisory Arton Capital, which put the United Arab Emirates in pole position. The ranking is based on data from the International Air Transport Association, which maintains the world's largest database of travel information, and it is enhanced by extensive, ongoing research by the Henley & Partners Research Department.

Nation celebrates National Youth Day on January 12

National Youth Day is celebrated every year on January 12 to mark the 160th birth anniversary of Swami Vivekananda. Every year on this occasion, the government organises National Youth Festival in collaboration with one state willing to host from January 12 to January 16. This year Prime Minister Narendra Modi inaugurate the festival on January 12 in Huballi, Karnataka.

The basic objective of National Youth Day is to bring the youth of the country together in an attempt to showcase their talents in various activities to cover almost all sociocultural aspects of life, providing an opportunity to amateur young artists to express themselves and interact with fellow artists and to further learn the new art forms from experts of various disciplines.

Theme of National Youth Festival

The Centre said the festival is held to provide exposure to youths at a national level and this year's theme for the fourday programme is "Viksit Yuva - Viksit Bharat (Developed Youth - Developed India)".

This year host state of National Youth Festival

This year the festival is being organized by the Union Ministry of Youth Affairs & Sports in collaboration with the Karnataka. The event will be held from January 12 to January 16, 2023, at Hubballi- Dharwad, Karnataka. More than 30,000 youth will attend the inaugural function where the Prime Minister will share his vision with them. During this unique five-day event, over 7500 youth delegates from all over India, recognized and leaders in their own field of activity, get together to engage in different learning activities.

History of National Youth Day

In the year 1985, the government had declared the birth anniversary of Swami Vivekananda, January 12, as 'National Youth Day'. Since then, all the centres of Ramakrishna Math and Ramakrishna Mission have been celebrating the occasion through various programmes.

About Swami Vivekananda

- Swami Vivekananda, born Narendranath Datta on January 12, 1863, was a disciple of Sri 19th-century Indian mystic Ramakrishna Paramhansa. He went on to become a key figure in the introduction of the Indian darsanas (teachings, practices) of Vedanta and Yoga to the Western world and was credited with raising interfaith awareness.
- Vivekanand was highly regarded as a major force in the contemporary Hindu reform movements in India and contributed to the concept of nationalism in colonial India. - Famous for his famous speech in Parliament of World's Religions in Chicago, 1893, he focused on channelling the energy of the youth.
- As his teachings and practices had a huge influence on the youth, the Government of India in 1984 declared January 12 day as National Youth Day.

Miss Universe 2022

The United States candidate R'Bonney Gabriel has crowned Miss Universe 2022 at a ceremony held in New Orleans, Mexico. The crown was presented to her by India's Harnaaz Kaur Sandhu who had won the 2021 title. She was handed a bouquet of flowers, draped in the winner's sash and crowned with a tiara onstage at the 71st Miss Universe Competition. The second runner-up was Miss Dominican Republic, Andreina Martinez. Miss Curacao, Gabriela Dos Santos, and Miss Puerto Rico, Ashley Carino, rounded out the top five finalists.

Indian participant

Divita Rai of India reached the top 16, but she was unable to advance further. India's participation in the 71st Miss Universe was restricted to the top 16 since she was unable to make it into the top 5.

Critics Choice Awards 2023

28th Critics Choice Awards

The 28th Critics Choice Awards were held, and once again, SS Rajamouli's RRR has made India proud, as the film scored two awards. RRR won Best Song award for Naatu Naatu, as well as Best Foreign Language film. RRR was also nominated for Best Director, Best Picture and Best Visual Effects.

The Critics Choice Movie award Formerly known as the Broadcast Film Critics Association award was held. Critics Choice Awards Winner 2023 shows were hosted by Chelsea Handler.

Critics Choice Movie Awards

The Critics Choice Movie awards were given according to the nominees selected. You can see the Critics' Choice Movie awards list in the given. The list is given according to the movie, series etc.

- Best Animated Series: "Harley Quinn"
- Best Foreign Language Series: "Pachinko"
- Best Comedy Special: "Norm Macdonald: Nothing Special"
- Best Talk Show: "Last Week Tonight With John Oliver"
- SeeHer Award: Janelle Monáe
- Lifetime Achievement Award: Jeff Bridges
- Best Picture: "Everything Everywhere All at Once"
- Best Director: Daniel Kwan and Daniel Scheinert, "Everything Everywhere All at Once"
- Best Actor: Brendan Fraser, "The Whale"
- Best Actress: Cate Blanchett, "Tár"
- Best Supporting Actor: Ke Huy Quan, "Everything Everywhere All at Once"
- Best Supporting Actress: Angela Bassett, "Black Panther: Wakanda Forever"
- Best Young Actor or Actress: Gabriel LaBelle, "The Fabelmans"
- Best Acting Ensemble: "Glass Onion: A Knives Out Mystery"
- Best Original Screenplay: Daniel Kwan and Daniel Scheinert, "Everything Everywhere All at Once"

- Best Adapted Screenplay: Sarah Polley, "Women Talking"
- Best Cinematography: Claudio Miranda, "Top Gun: Maverick"
- Best Production Design: Florencia Martin and Anthony Carlino, "Babylon"
- Best Editing: Paul Rogers, "Everything Everywhere All at Once"

Critics Choice Super Award 2023

The Critics choose super award 2023 for the films and the television series you can see in the given below. In this above section you see the various actors and their award. But now you can see the Indian movie and the best song award which goes to an RRR movie. The movie was made by SS Rajamouli. The list of the Critics Choice Super award 2023 is given below as you can see it.

- Best Foreign Language Film: "RRR"
- Best Song: "Naatu Naatu," "RRR"
- Best Score: Hildur Gudnadóttir, "Tár"

Television

- Best Drama Series: "Better Call Saul"
- Best Actor in a Drama Series: Bob Odenkirk, "Better Call Saul"
- Best Actress in a Drama Series: Zendaya, "Euphoria"
- Best Supporting Actor in a Drama Series: Giancarlo Esposito, "Better Call Saul"
- Best Supporting Actress in a Drama Series: Jennifer Coolidge, "The White Lotus"
- Best Comedy Series: "Abbott Elementary"

Other Category

- SeeHer Award: Janelle Monáe
- Lifetime Achievement Award: Jeff Bridges

Amazon back as World's Most Valued Brand, Apple down to No 2

Billionaire Jeff Bezos's e-commerce company Amazon has become the most valued brand, overtaking Apple, last year's topper. Amazon has reclaimed the top spot as the world's most valuable brand despite its brand value falling 15 per cent this year from $350.3 billion to $299.3 billion. According to brand valuation consultancy Brand Finance's report, "Global 500 2023", while Amazon is back at No 1, its brand value has fallen by over $50 billion this year, with its rating slipping from AAA+ to AAA. This is as consumers evaluate it more harshly in the post-pandemic world.

Apple slipped to the second spot

iPhone maker Apple slipped to the second slot to be ranked the world's second most valuable brand (brand value down 16% to $297.5 billion from $355.1 billion). This year's fall in brand value relates to a fall in forecast revenue with supply chain disruptions and a constrained labour market expected to limit the supply of its marquee hardware products. Among all, 48 tech brands featured in the ranking, which is two less than the earlier 50 rated in 2022. This is after Snapchat and Twitter dropped out.

List of the Top 10 most valuable brands according to the report

- Amazon- Worth $299.3 billion
- Apple- Worth $297.5 billion
- Google-Worth $281.4 billion
- Microsoft-Worth $191.6 billion
- Walmart-Worth $113.8 billion
- Samsung Group-Worth $99.7 billion
- ICBC-Worth $69.5 billion
- Verizon-Worth $67.4 billion
- Tesla-Worth $66.2 billion
- TikTok/Douyin-Worth $65.7 billion

India's Top-Valued Brands

From India, over 150-year-old Tata Group is the only brand to feature in the top 100. The conglomerate's brand value jumped up to 69 from 78 last year. However, reasons for the ranking going up were not available. Among Indian IT tech giants, Infosys jumped to the 150th slot from 158 last year. According to the report, Infosys has seen an 84% increase in its brand value since 2020.

Brand Guardianship Index 2023

Billionaire Mukesh Ambani ranked No.1 among Indians and second globally on the Brand Guardianship Index 2023, overtaking the likes of Satya Nadella of Microsoft and Google's Sundar Pichai. Nvidia CEO Jensen Huang topped the list globally, with Microsoft's Satya Nadella occupying third place.

S.NO	CEO	CORPORATION
1	Jensen Huang	Nvidia
2	Mukesh Ambani	Reliance
3	Satya Nadella	Microsoft
4	Shantanu Narayen	Adobe
5	Sundar Pichai	Google
6	Punit Renjen	Deloitte
7	Fabrizio Freda	Estee Lauder Companies
8	Natarajan Chandrasekaran	Tata
9	Piyush Gupta	DBS
10	Huateng Ma	Tencent

About Brand Guardianship Index

- The Brand Guardianship Index by Brand Finance, a leading global independent brand consultancy, is a global recognition of CEOs, who are building business value in a sustainable manner, by balancing the needs of all stakeholders - employees, investors, and the wider society.
- The Brand Guardianship Index includes 'equity' factors, which reflect current perceptions, 'performance' factors which reflect the tangible results of these perceptions, and 'Investment' factors which support future performance.

About Brand Finance

Brand Finance is the world's leading independent brand valuation and strategy consultancy. Headquartered in the City of London, we are present in over 20 countries. Founded in 1996 with the aim of 'bridging the gap between marketing and finance', for more than 20 years we have helped companies and organisations of all types to connect their brands to the bottom line.

Parakram Diwas 2023

Netaji Subhas Chandra Bose Jayanti or Netaji Jayanti is a national event celebrated in India as Parakram Diwas on January 23 to mark the birth of prominent Indian freedom fighter Netaji Subhas Chandra Bose. This year nation celebrates 126th birth anniversary of Netaji Subhas Chandra Bose. For the first time, Netaji Jayanti was celebrated as Parakram Divas in 2021 on the occasion of his 124th birthday. In West Bengal, Jharkhand, Tripura, and Assam, it is a recognised holiday. On this day, the Indian government honours Netaji.

Importance of Parakram Diwas

The purpose of the holiday is to recall and honour Netaji's tremendous devotion to the country and his unwavering spirit. He was crucial to the cause for Indian independence. Netaji was a prominent nationalist, politician, and freedom fighter. This day has been designated to encourage Indians, especially young people, to aspire to his strength, perseverance, selflessness, and patriotic fervour despite oppression. He oversaw the Indian National Army (Azad Hind Fouj). He was the founder-head of the Azad Hind Government.

ICC Men's and Women's T20I Team of The Year 2022

ICC Men's T20I team 2022

Jos Buttler (C), Mohammad Rizwan, Virat Kohli, Suryakumar Yadav, Glenn Phillips, Sikandar Raza, Hardik Pandya, Sam Curran, Wanindu Hasaranga, Haris Rauf, Josh Little.

ICC Women's T20I team 2022

Smriti Mandhana, Beth Mooney, Sophie Devine (C), Ash Gardner, Tahlia McGrath, Nida Dar, Deepti Sharma, Richa Ghosh (wk), Sophie Ecclestone, Renuka Singh.

Padma Awards 2023 Winners

The Government of India has announced the Padma Awards 2023 Winners List. According to the Padma Awards website, the Padma Awards are India's highest civilian honors after the Bharat Ratna, seeking to "recognize achievements in all fields of activities or disciplines where an element of public service is involved". These Awards are distributed by the President of India at ceremonial functions which are held at Rashtrapati Bhawan usually around March/ April every year. For the year 2023, the President has approved conferment of 106 Padma Awards including 3 duo cases (in a duo case, the Award is counted as one) as per list below. The list comprises 6 Padma Vibhushan, 9 Padma Bhushan and 91 Padma Shri Awards. 19 of the awardees are women and the list also includes 2 persons from the category of Foreigners/Non Resident India (NRI)/Person of Indian Origin (PIO) /Overseas Citizen Of India (OCI) and 7 Posthumous awardees.

Notably

Padma Vibhushan (for exceptional and distinguished service), Padma Bhushan (distinguished service of higher order) and Padma Shri (distinguished service).

Padma Awards 2023 Highlights

- ORS icon Dilip Mahalanabis (Medicine), Samajwadi Party founder and former Uttar Pradesh Chief Minister Mulayam Singh Yadav (Public Affairs), and architect Balakrishna Doshi (Others-Architecture) have been picked to be awarded Padma Vibhushan posthumously.
- Mahalanabis pioneered the wide use of ORS (Oral Rehydration Solution) which is estimated to have saved more than 5 crore lives globally. Mahalanabis demonstrated the effectiveness of ORS while serving in Refugee camps during the 1971 Bangladesh Liberation War, having returned from USA to serve.

Padma Vibhushan Winners List

Name	Field	State / Country
Shri Balkrishna Doshi (Posthumous)	Others – Architecture	Gujarat
Shri Zakir Hussain	Art	Maharashtra
Shri S M Krishna	Public Affairs	Karnataka

Shri Dilip Mahala Nabis (Posthumous)	Medicine	West Bengal
Shri Srinivas Varadhan	Science & Engineering	United States of America
Shri Mulayam Singh Yadav (Posthumous)	Public Affairs	Uttar Pradesh

Padma Bhushan Winners List

Name	Field	State / Country
Shri S L Bhyrappa	Literature & Education	Karnataka
Shri Kumar Mangalam Birla	Trade & Industry	Maharashtra
Shri Deepak Dhar	Science & Engineering	Maharashtra
Ms. Vani Jairam	Art	Tamil Nadu
Swami Chinna Jeeyar	Others – Spiritualism	Telangana
Ms. Suman Kalyanpur	Art	Maharashtra
Shri Kapil Kapoor	Literature & Education	Delhi
Ms. Sudha Murty	Social Work	Karnataka
Shri Kamlesh D Patel	Others – Spiritualism	Telangana

Padma Sri Winners List

Name	Field	State / Country
Dr. Sukama Acharya	Others – Spiritualism	Haryana

Ms. Jodhaiyabai Baiga	Art	Madhya Pradesh
Shri Premjit Baria	Art	Dadra and Nagar Haveli and Daman and Diu
Ms. Usha Barle	Art	Chhattisgarh
Shri Munishwar Chanddawar	Medicine	Madhya Pradesh
Shri Hemant Chauhan	Art	Gujarat
Shri Bhanubhai Chitara	Art	Gujarat
Ms. Hemoprova Chutia	Art	Assam
Shri Narendra Chandra Debbarma (Posthumous)	Public Affairs	Tripura
Ms. Subhadra Devi	Art	Bihar
Shri Khadar Valli Dudekula	Science & Engineering	Karnataka
Shri Hem Chandra Goswami	Art	Assam
Ms. Pritikana Goswami	Art	West Bengal
Shri Radha Charan Gupta	Literature & Education	Uttar Pradesh
Shri Modadugu Vijay Gupta	Science & Engineering	Telangana
Shri Ahmed Hussain & Shri Mohd Hussain (Duo)	Art	Rajasthan
Shri Dilshad Hussain	Art	Uttar Pradesh
Shri Bhiku Ramji Idate	Social Work	Maharashtra
Shri C I Issac	Literature & Education	Kerala

Shri Rattan Singh Jaggi	Literature & Education	Punjab
Shri Bikram Bahadur Jamatia	Social Work	Tripura
Shri Ramkuiwangbe Jene	Social Work	Assam
Shri Rakesh Radheshyam Jhunjhunwala (Posthumous)	Trade & Industry	Maharashtra
Shri Ratan Chandra Kar	Medicine	Andaman & Nicobar Islands
Shri Mahipat Kavi	Art	Gujarat
Shri M M Keeravaani	Art	Andhra Pradesh
Shri Areez Khambatta (Posthumous)	Trade & Industry	Gujarat
Shri Parshuram Komaji Khune	Art	Maharashtra
Shri Ganesh Nagappa Krishnarajanagara	Science & Engineering	Andhra Pradesh
Shri Maguni Charan Kuanr	Art	Odisha
Shri Anand Kumar	Literature & Education	Bihar
Shri Arvind Kumar	Science & Engineering	Uttar Pradesh
Shri Domar Singh Kunvar	Art	Chhattisgarh
Shri Risingbor Kurkalang	Art	Meghalaya
Ms. Hirabai Lobi	Social Work	Gujarat
Shri Moolchand Lodha	Social Work	Rajasthan
Ms. Rani Machaiah	Art	Karnataka

Shri Ajay Kumar Mandavi	Art	Chhattisgarh
Shri Prabhakar Bhanudas Mande	Literature & Education	Maharashtra
Shri Gajanan Jagannath Mane	Social Work	Maharashtra
Shri Antaryami Mishra	Literature & Education	Odisha
Shri Nadoja Pindipapanahalli Munivenkatappa	Art	Karnataka
Prof. (Dr.) Mahendra Pal	Science & Engineering	Gujarat
Shri Uma Shankar Pandey	Social Work	Uttar Pradesh
Shri Ramesh Parmar & Ms. Shanti Parmar (Duo)	Art	Madhya Pradesh
Dr. Nalini Parthasarathi	Medicine	Puducherry
Shri Hanumantha Rao Pasupuleti	Medicine	Telangana
Shri Ramesh Patange	Literature & Education	Maharashtra
Ms. Krishna Patel	Art	Odisha
Shri K Kalyanasundaram Pillai	Art	Tamil Nadu
Shri V P Appukuttan Poduval	Social Work	Kerala
Shri Kapil Dev Prasad	Art	Bihar
Shri S R D Prasad	Sports	Kerala
Shri Shah Rasheed Ahmed Quadri	Art	Karnataka
Shri C V Raju	Art	Andhra Pradesh

Shri Bakshi Ram	Science & Engineering	Haryana
Shri Cheruvayal K Raman	Others – Agriculture	Kerala
Ms. Sujatha Ramdorai	Science & Engineering	Canada
Shri Abbareddy Nageswara Rao	Science & Engineering	Andhra Pradesh
Shri Pareshbhai Rathwa	Art	Gujarat
Shri B Ramakrishna Reddy	Literature & Education	Telangana
Shri Mangala Kanti Roy	Art	West Bengal
Ms. K C Runremsangi	Art	Mizoram
Shri Vadivel Gopal & Shri Masi Sadaiyan (Duo)	Social Work	Tamil Nadu
Shri Manoranjan Sahu	Medicine	Uttar Pradesh
Shri Patayat Sahu	Others – Agriculture	Odisha
Shri Ritwik Sanyal	Art	Uttar Pradesh
Shri Kota Satchidananda Sastry	Art	Andhra Pradesh
Shri Sankurathri Chandra Sekhar	Social Work	Andhra Pradesh
Shri K Shanathoiba Sharma	Sports	Manipur
Shri Nekram Sharma	Others – Agriculture	Himachal Pradesh
Shri Gurcharan Singh	Sports	Delhi
Shri Laxman Singh	Social Work	Rajasthan

Shri Mohan Singh	Literature & Education	Jammu & Kashmir
Shri Thounaojam Chaoba Singh	Public Affairs	Manipur
Shri Prakash Chandra Sood	Literature & Education	Andhra Pradesh
Ms. Neihunuo Sorhie	Art	Nagaland
Dr. Janum Singh Soy	Literature & Education	Jharkhand
Shri Kushok Thiksey Nawang Chamba Stanzin	Others – Spiritualism	Ladakh
Shri S Subbaraman	Others – Archaeology	Karnataka
Shri Moa Subong	Art	Nagaland
Shri Palam Kalyana Sundaram	Social Work	Tamil Nadu
Ms. Raveena Ravi Tandon	Art	Maharashtra
Shri Vishwanath Prasad Tiwari	Literature & Education	Uttar Pradesh
Shri Dhaniram Toto	Literature & Education	West Bengal
Shri Tula Ram Upreti	Others – Agriculture	Sikkim
Dr. Gopalsamy Veluchamy	Medicine	Tamil Nadu
Dr. Ishwar Chander Verma	Medicine	Delhi
Ms. Coomi Nariman Wadia	Art	Maharashtra
Shri Karma Wangchu (Posthumous)	Social Work	Arunachal Pradesh

Shri Ghulam Muhammad Zaz	Art	Jammu & Kashmir

About the Padma Awards

Instituted in 1954, these civilian awards, are generally announced on the occasion of Republic Day every year, and these awards seek to recognize 'work of distinction' and is given for distinguished and exceptional achievements/service in all fields/disciplines, such as, Art, Literature and Education, Sports, Medicine, Social Work, Science and Engineering, Public Affairs, Civil Service, Trade and Industry etc.

All nominations received for Padma Awards are placed before the Padma Awards Committee, which is constituted by the Prime Minister every year. The Padma Awards Committee is headed by the Cabinet Secretary and includes Home Secretary, Secretary to the President and four to six eminent persons as members. The recommendations of the committee are submitted to the Prime Minister and the President of India for approval.

Republic Day 2023

There are various events held for the first time in Republic day parade 2023

- For the first time in India's independent history, the iconic 21-Guns Salute to the President during the parade will use 105 mm Indian Field Guns replacing the Britishmade 25-Pounder guns. This year, only Made-in-India weapon systems, showcased at the Republic Day parade, keeping with the theme of "Atmanirbhar Bharat".
- For the first time, 12 women riders are participate of the Camel Contingent of the Border Security Force (BSF) and among the 16 marching contingents from the armed forces, Central Para Military Forces, Delhi Police, National Cadet Corps (NCC), NSS along with 19 military pipes and drums bands in the Republic Day parade this year.
- A team of "Daredevils" motor cycle riders from Corps of Signals co-led by a woman officer is the part of the parade. Lieutenant Dimple Bhati from the Corps of Signals, part of the Indian Army's Daredevils motorcycle team at the Republic

Day parade this year. The women officer had been training with the team for the last one year.

- The newly-recruited Agniveers also be a part of the parade for the first time.
- In a first, the Narcotics Control Bureau (NCB) will display a tableau during the Republic Day parade. 'Nasha Mukt Bharat', and a group of people standing in front of it, wearing different costumes of India and holding their arms out, with a banner placed below bearing a line “Together We Can Do It”.
- Marching down the Kartavya Path for the first time, the combined Band and Marching contingent of the Egyptian Armed Forces, led by Colonel Mahmoud Mohamed Abdel Fattah El Kharasawy. The contingent consist of 144 soldiers, representing the main branches of the Egyptian Armed Forces.
- The Indian Navy's IL-38, showcased during the parade for the first and last time, IL-38 has served Indian Navy for 42 years.
- The biggest drone show in India, comprising 3,500 indigenous drones, light up the evening sky over the Raisina hills during Beating the Retreat ceremony on January 29th.
- For the first time, a 3-D anamorphic projection, organised during the Beating the Retreat Ceremony on the facade of the North and South Block.
- Garud Special Forces of the Indian Air Force are participating for the first time in the Republic Day parade. Squadron Leader Pritam Singh Jaitawat leading the Garud team as part of the IAF contingent.
- Uttarakhand tableau wins first prize Uttarakhand tableau which showcased the state's wildlife and religious sites at the 74th Republic Day parade has won the top prize. Uttarakhand's tableau showcased the state's wildlife and religious sites during the ceremonial parade at Kartavya Path on January 26.
- In the foreground of the tableau, reindeer, deer and various birds were shown roaming in the world-famous Corbett National Park. The central part of the tableau depicted the state animal of Uttarakhand, musk deer, national bird peacock and ghoral.

- Jageshwar Dham, a group of 125 small and big ancient temples in Manaskhand's Almora district, and popular deodar trees were shown in the rear part of the tableau.
- Uttarakhand won the first prize for its tableau, followed by Maharashtra and Uttar Pradesh in the second and third positions respectively.
- The tableau of Maharashtra on Azadi ka Amrit Mahotsav presented "Sade Tin Shaktipithe" and "Nari Shakti", while that of Uttar Pradesh showcased Ayodhya Deepotsav.
- Gujarat's tableau emerged as the numero uno in the popular choice segment.
- Army's Punjab Regiment has been adjudged the best marching contingent among the three services, while the Central Reserve Police Force's (CRPF) marching contingent won the top prize among the CAPFs and other auxiliary forces.
- Among the ministries and departments, the tableau of the Ministry of Tribal Affairs (Eklavya Model Residential Schools) won the best prize.
- The Central Public Works Department's tableau on biodiversity conservation and 'Vande Bharatam' dance group earned a special prize.
- The IAF's marching contingent emerged as the winner among the three services in the popular choice category.
- Among the tableaux from states and union territories, Gujarat won the first prize in the category, followed by Uttar Pradesh and Maharashtra in that order. Kutchi embroidery and decoration, known for its mirror work, traditional 'bhungas' and renewable energy production were the focus elements in the Gujarat tableau. The village of Modhera, famous for its Sun Temple, and being India's first round-the-clock solar-powered village was also showcased in the tableau.
- Among the central ministries and departments, the tableau by the CAPF, the Ministry of Home Affairs, emerged as the best in the popular choice segment.

How these tableau selected?

Three panels of judges were appointed for assessing the performance of the marching contingents from the three services, those from Central Armed Police Forces (CAPF) and other auxiliary forces, and tableaux from various states and union territories, and various ministries and departments. Citizens voted in an online poll on MyGov for their favourite tableaux and marching contingents in the popular choice category. The poll for the popular choice was conducted between January 25 and 28.

ICC annual awards 2022

The International Cricket Council (ICC) has announced its first individual award winners in the ICC Awards 2022, naming the stars honoured in the Associate, Emerging and T20I categories following a global vote conducted among the specialist panel of media representatives, the ICC Voting Academy and global fans who voted for their favourite stars. Winners in the 13 individual categories were based on overall performances and achievements throughout the calendar year, with winners announced across ICC digital channels.

ICC awards winners for 2022

- Sir Garfield Sobers Trophy: Babar Azam (Pakistan)
- Rachael Heyhoe Flint Trophy: Nat Sciver (England)
- Men's Test Cricketer of the Year: Ben Stokes (England)
- Men's ODI Cricketer of the Year: Babar Azam
- Women's ODI Cricketer of the Year: Nat Sciver
- Men's T20 International Cricketer of the Year: Suryakumar Yadav (India)
- Women's T20 International Cricketer of the Year: Tahlia McGrath (Australia)
- Men's Emerging Cricketer of the Year: Marco Jansen (South Africa)
- Women's Emerging Cricketer of the Year: Renuka Singh (India)
- Men's Associate Cricketer of the Year: Gerhard Erasmus (Namibia)
- Women's Associate Cricketer of the Year: Esha Oza (India)
- David Shepherd Trophy: Richard Illingworth (England)
- Spirit of Cricket Award: Aasif Sheikh (Nepal)

Gallantry Awards

President of India, Droupadi Murmu has approved 412 Gallantry awards and other Defence decorations to Armed Forces personnel and others. These include six Kirti

Chakras, including four posthumous, and 15 Shaurya Chakras including two posthumous. These include one Bar to Sena Medal (Gallantry), 92 Sena Medals, including four posthumous, one Nao Sena Medal (Gallantry), seven Vayu Sena Medals (Gallantry) and 29 Param Vishisht Seva Medals. President has also awarded President's Tatrakshak Medal and Tatrakshak Medal to Indian Coast Guard Personnel for their act of conspicuous gallantry, exceptional devotion to duty and distinguished service.

Kirti Chakra Awardees

- Major Shubhang of the Dogra Regiment from Indian Army
- Naik Jitendra Singh of the Rajput Regiment from Indian Army
- Jammu and Kashmir police constable Rohit Kumar (Posthumous)
- Sub Inspector Deepak Bhardwaj (Posthumous)
- Head constable Sodhi Narayan (Posthumous)
- Head constable Shrawan Kashyap (Posthumous)

Shaurya Chakra Awardees

- Major Aditya Bhadauria, Kumaon Regiment, Indian Army
- Captain Arun Kumar, Kumaun Regiment, Indian Army
- Captain Yudhvir Singh, mechanised infantry, Indian Army
- Captain Rakesh TR, Parachute Regiment, Indian Army
- Naik Jasbir Singh, Jammu and Kashmir Rifles, Indian Army (Posthumous)
- Naik Vikas Choudhary, Jammu and Kashmir Rifles, (Posthumous)
- Constable Mudasir Ahmad Sheikh, Jammu and Kashmir Police
- Group Captain Yogeshwar Krishnarao Kandalkar, Air Force
- Flight Lieutenant Tejpal, Air Force
- Squadron leader Sandeep Kumar Jhajhria, Air Force
- Corporal Anand Singh, Air Force
- Leading aircraftman Sunil Kumar, Air Force
- Assistant Commandant Satendra Singh
- Deputy Commandant Vikki Kumar Pandey
- Constable Vijay Oraon

Bar to Sena Medal (Gallantry)

- Major Rakesh Kumar, Indian Army

Nao Sena Medal (Gallantry)

- Late CDR Nishant Singh (Posthumous), Navy

Vayu Sena Medal (Gallantry)

- Wing Commander Sumedh Ashok Jamkar, Air Force
- Squadron leader Krishna Kumar Singh, Air Force
- Junior Warrant officer Srikanth Bonam, Air Force
- Sergeant Pankaj Kumar Rana, Air Force
- Corporal Satendra Kumar, Air Force
- Corporal Anthony Mang Kham, Air Force
- Leading Aircraftman Ravinder Singh, Air Force

Uttam Yudh Sewa Medal

- Lieutenant General Ram Chander Tiwari, Indian Army
- Lieutenant General Anindiya Sengupta, Indian Army
- Lieutenant General Amardeep Singh Aujla, Indian Army

President's Tatrakshak Medal (Distinguished Service)

- IG Anand Prakash Badola, TM (0248-M)

Tatrakshak Medal (Gallantry)

- ComdtDurgesh Chandra Tiwari
- Rishi, P/Nvk(R)
- Mohit Kumar Yadav, U/Nvk (RP)

Tatrakshak Medal

- DIG HimanshuNautiyal
- Sant Lal, P/Adh(RO)

Australian Open 2023

Novak Djokovic defeated Stefanos Tsitsipas in the final of men's singles match of the Australian Open 2023. Djokovic wins 10th Australian Open and 22nd grand slam. He levels Rafael Nadal with his 22nd Grand Slam title. In the Women's Singles category, Aryna Sabalenka defeated Elena Rybakina in the final, $4-6, 6-3, 6-4$ to win the women's singles tennis title at the 2023 Australian Open.

The 2023 Australian Open was a Grand Slam level tennis tournament held at Melbourne Park, from 16-29 January 2023. It was the 111th edition of the Australian Open, the 55th in the Open Era, and the first major of the year. There is a total prize pot of AUD $76.5 million (around £43.3 m) for the Australian Open 2023.

Table showing Winners in all categories

Category	Winner	Runner-Up
Men's Singles	N. Djokovic (Serbia)	Stefanos Tsitsipas (Greece)
Women's Singles	A. Sabalenka (Belarus)	E. Rybakina (Kazakhstan)
Men's Doubles	J. Kubler & R. Hijikata (Australia)	H. Nys (Monaco) & J. Zieliński (Poland)
Women's Doubles	B. Krejčíková & K. Siniaková (Czechia)	S. Aoyama & E. Shibahara (Japan)
Mixed Doubles	L. Stefani & R. Matos (Brazil)	R. Bopanna & S. Mirza (India)

History of Australian Open

Australian Open, one of the world's major tennis championships (the first of the four annual Grand Slam events), held at the National Tennis Centre at Melbourne Park in Melbourne, Australia. The Australian Open is managed by Tennis Australia, formerly the Lawn Tennis Association of Australia (LTAA) and was first played at the Warehouseman's Cricket Ground in Melbourne in November 1905 and the first for women in 1922. The facility is now known as the Albert Reserve Tennis Centre and was a grass court.

Banking and Financial Current Affairs

- The Reserve Bank of India's Medium-term Strategy Framework for the period 2023-2025 - 'Utkarsh 2.0' was launched by Shri Shaktikanta Das, Governor, RBI. The first strategy framework (Utkarsh 2022) covering the period 2019-2022 was launched in July 2019. It became a medium-term strategy document guiding the Bank's progress towards realisation of the identified milestones. Utkarsh 2.0 would allow the central bank to both react and act proactively to confront socio-economic challenges.

- Public sector bank Punjab and Sind Bank (PSB) has partnered with SBI Card to launch co-brand credit cards for the bank's customers. PSB has also entered the credit card market as a new product segment in its portfolio as a result of this collaboration. Three card variants-the PSB SBI Card ELITE, PSB SBI Card PRIME, and PSB SimplySAVE SBI Card-have been launched by both partners. This collaboration also marks the entry of PSB into 'credit cards' as a new product segment under the bank's portfolio. - The Reserve Bank of India said SBI, ICICI Bank, HDFC Bank remain domestic systemically important banks (D-SIBs). D-SIBs are those interconnected entities whose failure can impact the whole of the financial system and create instability. In addition to the usual capital conservation buffer, D-SIBs will need to maintain additional Common Equity Tier 1 (CET1).

- HDFC Bank, India's largest private sector bank, is partnering with Microsoft in the next phase of its digital transformation journey and unlocking business value by transforming the application portfolio, modernizing the data landscape and securing the enterprise with Microsoft Cloud. HDFC Bank as a part of its Future Ready strategy is developing in house IPs as well as partnering with several companies including FinTechs' to co -create technology IPs.

- The Reserve Bank of India has launched the Inflation Expectations Survey of Households (IESH) which will provide useful inputs for monetary policy. In the January 2023 round, the survey will be conducted across 19 cities. It aims to capture subjective assessments of price movements and inflation, based on individual consumption baskets.

- Bandhan Bank launched the 'Jahaan Bandhan, Wahaan Trust' campaign along with the bank's brand ambassador Sourav Ganguly. 'Jahaan Bandhan, Wahaan Trust' is an integrated marketing campaign in which the company has emphasized the 'trust' that the brand has been able to earn in a span of seven years as a bank.

- Issues related to ATM/debit cards and mobile/electronic banking were the top grounds of complaints received at the Office of Banking Ombudsman (OB0), said an RBI report. The coverage of RBIOS was extended to include the non-scheduled Urban Cooperative Banks (UCBs) with a deposit size of Rs 50 crore or above as at the end of the previous Financial Year. Credit Information Companies (CICs) were brought under RBI-IOS with effect from September 1, 2022. Between November 12, 2021 and March 31, 2022, a total of 1,86,268 complaints were received under the RBIOS.

- Axis Bank has signed an agreement with the Indian Institute of Science (IISc), Bengaluru, to establish a Centre for Mathematics and Computing at the institute.

- Reserve Bank of India (RBI) issued the list of six credit rating agencies that banks can use for the purpose of risk weighting banks' claims for capital adequacy purposes. The six credit rating agencies are Acuite Ratings & Research Limited, Credit Analysis and Research Limited (CARE), CRISIL Ratings Limited, ICRA Limited, India Ratings and Research Private Limited (India Ratings) \ and INFOMERICS Valuation and Rating Pvt Ltd.

- The Union Cabinet has approved the incentive scheme for the promotion of RuPay Debit Cards and low-value BHIM-UPI transactions (person-to-merchant) for the current financial year. The approved incentive scheme for promotion of RuPay Debit Cards and low-value BHIM-UPI transactions (P2M) in FY 2022-23 has a financial outlay of Rs 2,600 crore.

- India was among the top five markets, globally, in terms of equity fundraising despite the quantum of funds raised declining by 43 per cent. According to a report by Kotak Investment Banking, funds to the tune of $16.4 billion were transacted via equity capital market (ECM) activity in India in 2022. India's outperformance comes on the back of a sharper decline in ECM activity in major markets such as the United Kingdom, Australia and Japan. ECM activity globally took a hit on account of heightened volatility amid rising interest rates.

- State Bank of India (SBI) has launched e-Bank Guarantee (e-BG) facility in association with National e-Governance Services Limited (NeSL). India's largest lender said this facility will bring about a revolutionary change in the banking ecosystem, where bank guarantee is frequently used in large volumes. By using the NeSL's platform, the bank customers and other beneficiaries will instantly get an e-Bank Guarantee without additional verification.

- Sumitomo Mitsui Banking Corporation Group (SMBC Bank) of Japan and Oaktree Capital Management are among those that have submitted expressions of interest (EoIs) for the strategic stake sale in IDBI Bank. Oaktree is a US alternative assets firm founded by Howard Marks, one of the world's most formidable distressed debt investors. The stake being sold is held by the Centre and LIC.

- The Reserve Bank of India (RBI) said that the finances of Indian states are projected to improve in 2022-23 with the consolidated gross fiscal deficit to gross domestic product ratio seen falling to 3.4 percent from 4.1 percent for the previous year. The fiscal health of the states has improved from a sharp pandemicinduced deterioration in 2020-21 on the back of a broadbased economic recovery and resulting high revenue collections. During the pandemic years, states' finances were under pressure due to rising expenditures and limited revenue growth.

- The Reserve Bank of India tweaked norms related to acquisition and holding of shares in banks to ensure that their ultimate ownership and control remain well diversified and the major shareholders are 'fit and proper' on a continuing basis. The central bank has issued 'Master Direction - Reserve Bank of India (Acquisition and Holding of Shares or Voting Rights in Banking Companies) Directions, 2023'. The directions are applicable to all banking companies, including Local Area Banks (LABs), Small Finance Banks (SFBs) and Payments Banks (PBs) operating in India. - Paytm Payments Bank said it has received final approval from the Reserve Bank of India to operate as a Bharat Bill Payment 0perating Unit (BBPOU). Under Bharat Bill Payment System (BBPS), a BBPOU is allowed to facilitate bill payment services of electricity, phone, DTH, water, gas insurance, loan repayments, FASTag recharge, education fees, credit card bill and municipal taxes.

- Mastercard announced the expansion of its signature Girls4Tech, STEM (Science, Technology, Engineering, and Math) education program in India. The Girls4Tech is supported by Mastercard Impact Fund and in partnership with the American India Foundation (AIF).

- Tamilnad Mercantile Bank Limited (TMB) has bagged the Best Small Bank award in the Best Banks survey for the year 2022. The Best Banks survey was conducted by Business Today- KPMG (BT-KPMG Best Banks Survey). The bank has won the Best Small Bank Award under the category of banks with a book size of less than Rs 1 Lakh crore.

- The Reserve Bank of India's 2023 monetary policy objective is to hold inflation within the mandated tolerance band and guide it towards the medium-term target of 4% by 2024, it said in its monthly bulletin published. Recent data indicated "the first milestone of monetary policy is being passed - bringing inflation into the tolerance band", the RBI said. The objective during 2023 is to tether inflation therein so that it aligns with the target by 2024 - the second milestone, it added.

- State-owned Punjab National Bank (PNB) offers credit cards against Fixed Deposit to customers who don't meet the eligibility criteria for regular credit cards. This facility will be available for salary account customers, and they shall be able to apply through the mobile banking app PNB One, website or Internet Banking Service (IBS), the lender said. Customers can avail loan without visiting a bank branch, adding there is a concession of 0.25 per cent on the interest rate when applied through digital platforms like PNB One.

- The Reserve Bank of India (RBI) has proposed a new set of rules governing loan loss provisioning by banks as it looks to enhance the resilience of the banking system. The central bank proposes to amend the regulations governing loan loss provisioning to incorporate a more forward looking "expected credit losses approach" as against the current "incurred loss" approach, the RBI says in a discussion paper. Canara Bank said it plans to sell its stake in Russian Joint Venture(JV) Commercial Indo Bank LLC (CIBL) to the other venture partner State Bank of India (SBI) for about Rs 114 crore. CIBL, incorporated in 2003, is a joint venture in Russia between SBI (60 per cent) and Canara Bank (40 per cent).

- The Indian government bought back bonds maturing in 2024 from the Reserve Bank of India, while also issuing bonds maturing in 2032 worth a similar quantum, the central bank said. The transaction was carried out using Financial Benchmarks India Pvt Ltd. (FBIL) prices. The government bought back 6.18% bonds maturing in 2024 worth 226.10 billion rupees ($2.78 billion) at a price of 98.62 rupees while it issued 8.28% 2032 bonds worth 210.26 billion rupees to the RBI at 106.05 rupees.

- AU Small Finance Bank, India's largest Small Finance Bank, announced the launch of a first-of-its-kind platform in the credit card industry - the SwipeUp platform. With this platform, AU Bank will provide an opportunity to other bank Credit Cardholders to upgrade their card to one of AU Credit Cards.

Economy Current Affairs

- According to a government announcement, India's goods and services tax receipts increased 15% year over year in December to Rs 1.49 lakh crore ($18.07 billion), suggesting robust economic activity throughout the holiday season. In November, revenue from goods and services taxes totaled Rs. 1.46 lakh crore.

- Unemployment rate in India rose to 8.30 per cent in December 2022, the highest in 16 months, according to data from Centre for Monitoring Indian Economy (CMIE). It was 8 per cent in the month of November. While urban unemployment rose to 10.09 per cent in December, from 8.96 per cent in November, rural unemployment moved to 7.44% from 7.55%, the data revealed.

- India's international financial assets declined by $56.5 billion during July-September 2022 with valuation losses accounting for a major part. Reserve assets remained the dominant component (62.9% share) of India's international financial assets. The net claims of non-residents on India increased by $34.3 billion during Q2 of FY23 and stood at $389.6 billion in September.

- India aims to cut spending on food and fertiliser subsidies to 3.7 trillion rupees ($44.6 billion) in the fiscal year from April, down 26% from this, to rein in a fiscal deficit that ballooned during the COVID-19 pandemic. Spending on fertiliser subsidies will likely fall to about Rs 1.4 lakh crore. That compares with nearly Rs 2.3 lakh crore this year.

- India's economy is expected to grow 7.0% in the current financial year, according to the first advance estimates by the National Statistical Office (NSO). New Delhi had pegged India's growth at 8.7% in the last fiscal year that ended March 31, 2022.

- In a major development, India has surpassed Japan in terms of auto sales last year to become the third-largest auto market globally for the first time. India's total sales of new vehicles stood at around 4.25 million units, based on preliminary results, topping the 4.2 million sold in Japan.

- India's growth is expected to slow to 6.9 per cent in Financial Year 2023, a 0.6 percentage point decrease since June, as the global economy and rising uncertainty weigh on export and investment growth, according to the World Bank. However, India is expected to be the fastest growing economy among the seven largest developing economies.

- The current interest rate on Kisan Vikas Patra (KVP) account deposits is 7.2% compounded annually. The revised rate was announced on December 30. This rate would apply to KVP deposits made in the first quarter of the New Year 2023. Amid rising inflation and repo rate hikes by the Reserve Bank of India, KVP depositors were expecting an upward revision in the interest rate.

- Retail inflation declined to a one-year low of 5.72 per cent in December 2022, mainly due to softening prices of food items. Also, it was well within the Reserve Bank of India's (RBI) comfort range of 2 per cent-6 per cent for a second month, data released by the Ministry of Statistics & Programme Implementation (MoSPI) showed. The Consumer Price Index (CPI)-based inflation rate eased to 5.72 per cent in December. It was 5.88 per cent in November, and 6.77 per cent in October 2022.

- The phased roll-out of E20 (20 per cent ethanol blending in gasoline) will begin on April 1, Petroleum Minister Hardeep Singh Puri has said. The fuel will be available at select outlets and will not require changes to car engines. The proposed roll-out will give further impetus to the government's plans of achieving the level of 20 per cent ethanol blending in the overall petrol supply in the country by ethanol supply year 2025-2026.

- Regulator SEBI allowed Alternative Investment Funds(AIFs) to participate in the Credit Default Swaps(CDS) market as protection buyers and sellers in a bid to facilitate the deepening of the domestic corporate bond segment. The new norms, which will come into force with immediate effect, allow business entities to hedge risks associated with the bonds market.

- In December 2022, the wholesale price-based inflation fell to 4.95 percent, primarily as a result of lower costs for food items and crude oil. Inflation measured by the Wholesale Price Index (WPI) was 5.85% in November 2022 and 14.27% in December 2021.

- The upcoming Indian budget for 2023-24 will be a challenging one for the government to follow the roadmap for fiscal consolidation amidst a global environment of declining inflation, said a top economist of State Bank of India in a report. For India, this could make things difficult to set a nominal gross domestic product (GDP) number significantly higher than 10 per cent, with a deflator about 3.5 per cent. But this could also mean a higher GDP growth than anticipated at about 6.2 per cent.

- World Bank forecast Pakistan's economic growth to slow further to two percent during the current year. This will mark a drop of two percentage points from its June 2022 estimates, according to the World Bank's Global Economic Prospects report. The report said that Pakistan's economic output was not only declining itself but also bringing down the regional growth rate as well. Forecasting Pakistan's GDP growth rate to improve to 3.2 per cent in 2024, the report said, "Policy uncertainty further complicates the economic outlook" of Pakistan.

- The country's services exports are doing "extremely well" and going by the current trend these outbound shipments would register about 20 per cent growth in this fiscal and cross the USD 300 billion target despite global economic uncertainties. With all these stress, where every global leader is talking of "very" tough times, India's exports rose 9 per cent year-on-year during April-December 2022-23.

- The United Nations (UN) has cut its GDP growth forecast for India for calendar year 2023 to 5.8 percent, citing the effect of tighter monetary policy and weak global demand. Growth in India is expected to remain strong at 5.8 percent, albeit slightly lower than the estimated 6.4 percent in 2022, as higher interest rates and a global slowdown weigh on investment and exports, the UN's World Economic Situation and Prospects 2023 report.

- Employees' Provident Fund Organisation (EPF0) has launched a massive district outreach program in all the districts of the country through a revamped Nidhi Aapke Nikat program. The aim of this program is to reach all the districts of the country on the same day i.e. 27th of every month. EPFO organized camps in 685 districts of the country. In the year 2015, Bhavishya Nidhi Adalat was rechristened as Nidhi Aapke Nikat and in the year 2019, the outreach of the Nidhi Aapke Nikat Program was further improved by inviting participation of trade unions. - India will become the first major economy to move to a T + 1 (trade plus one) market settlement cycle when it finally makes the transition on January 27. The Chinese market is currently partly T + 1. With the move, all stock settlements will be done the next day, making financial transactions faster in the stock market.

- India's forex reserves increased by $1.73 billion to $73.7 billion in the week ended Jan. 20, the Reserve Bank of India said. This is the second consecutive week of a rise in the kitty after the $10.4 billion jump to $572 billion during the preceding week. In October 2021, the country's forex kitty had reached an all-time high of $645 billion. The reserves have been declining as the central bank deploys the kitty to defend the rupee amid pressures caused majorly by global developments.

- Finance Minister Nirmala Sitharaman presented the economy survey to Parliament. According to the economic survey, India's economy will expand by 6.5 percent in 2023-2024 as opposed to 7 percent in the current fiscal year and 8.7 percent in 2021-2022. The Economic Survey 2022-23 is primarily the government's assessment of the economy's performance over the previous year.

- The International Monetary Fund (IMF) has informed it is expecting some setbacks in the Indian economy next fiscal year and projected the growth to 6.1 percent from 6.8 percent during the current fiscal ending March 31.

Business Current Affairs

- India's Unified Payments Interface (UPI) processed a record 7.82 billion transactions in December, worth a total of INR 12.82tn ($174.6bn). This represents an increase of 7.12% in volume and 7.73% in value compared to November. On a year-on-year basis, volume and value increased by 71% and 55% respectively.

- The net profit of operating public sector enterprises jumped 50.87 per cent to ₹2.49 lakh crore during 2021-22, with ONGC, Indian Oil Corp, Power Grid, NTPC and SAIL emerging as the top five performers. The net profit of operating central public sector enterprises (CPSEs) stood at ₹ 1.65 lakh crore in the previous fiscal.

- It is estimated that the Indian economy grew by 9.7% in the first half of 2022-23, significantly higher than China's 2.2%, the UK's 3.4% and the USA's 1.8%. The local banking sector is often a proxy to the trends in India's economy. Take the latest round of a survey by the Federation of Indian Chambers of Commerce and Industry (FICCI) and Indian Banks' Association (IBA). Conducted over the first half of 2022 across 25 lenders in India that account for three-quarters of the sector's assets, it reveals a fair degree of comfort. Unlike last year's majority, only a small fraction of surveyed banks reported rising requests for loan rejigs.

- Zerodha-backed GoldenPi Technologies has become the first online bond platform provider to receive a debt brokerage license from market regulator Securities and Exchange Board of India (Sebi). The Bengaluru-based fintech firm expects this development to spur greater trust in online bonds and debentures investment space.

- Fintech platform BharatPe received in-principle authorisation from the Reserve Bank of India (RBI) to operate as an online payment aggregator (PA). The company said that an in-principle nod was awarded to Resilient Payments Private Ltd, a 100 percent subsidiary of Resilient Innovations Private Ltd (BharatPe).

- India's fastest payment app PayRup was launched in India on 9th January 2023. PayRup is built with the finest technology of web 3.0. It provides an advanced digital payment experience with an outstanding user experience and can pay utility bills and landline bills, recharge their mobile, broadband, DTH, and purchase gift cards.

- China's Alibaba Group sold a 3.1% stake in Indian digital payments firm Paytm for a total of $125 million through a block deal. Shares of the company fell as much as 8.8% to 528 rupees in afternoon trading, and was last down 5.8%. Alibaba, which held a 6.26% stake in Paytm as of end-September, sold the stake at 536.95 rupees apiece. Paytm's stock has risen about 9% this year up to last close, after reporting strong preliminary figures for the third quarter.

- The National Payments Corporation of India (NPCI) has instructed members of the Unified Payments Interface (UPI) ecosystem to allow non-resident account types such as non-resident external (NRE)/ non-resident ordinary (NRO) accounts having international mobile numbers to get onboarded and transact through UPI. To begin with, NPCI will be enabling transactions from mobile numbers having country codes of Singapore, Australia, Canada, Hong Kong, Oman, Qatar, USA, Saudi Arabia, United Arab Emirates, and the United Kingdom, along with the current domestic country code.

- In a major boost to the film and entertainment industry, PVR-Inox merger has been approved by the National Company Law Tribunal. The NCLT judge has approved the scheme of merger in a verbal order. A written order is likely to be passed in the next 15 – 20 days.
- Adani Enterprises has an agreement with Ashok Leyland, India, and Ballard Power, Canada to launch a pilot project to develop a hydrogen fuel cell electric truck (FCET) for mining logistics and transportation. The collaboration between Adani Enterprises and Ashok Leyland, India, and Ballard Power, Canada marks Asia's first planned hydrogen-powered mining truck.
- Google is actively working on a Soundbox for the India market, similar to the Paytm or PhonePe ones that you see at your neighbourhood shop which gives a sound alert on the digital payment that has been made. The search giant is piloting a soundbox of its own in the country to alert sellers of confirmations for Unified Payments Interface (UPI)-based payments.
- Bharti Airtel Group announced that it will be investing Rs 2,000 crore in setting up a large hyperscale data centre in Hyderabad. The announcement was made at the Telangana Lounge at Davos, Switzerland in the presence of Telangana Minister for IT and Industries KT Rama Rao.
- The Life Insurance Corporation of India (LIC) has launched LIC Jeevan Azad Plan. It is a limited period premium payment plan that offers financial support for the family in case of unfortunate death of the life assured during the policy term. If the LIC policyholder survives the maturity term, then the plan offers a guaranteed base sum-assured amount.
- Payments and financial services unicorn PhonePe has raised $350 million in funding from General Atlantic, a leading global growth equity firm, at a premoney valuation of $12 billion, making the Walmartowned start-up the most-valued financial technology (fintech) player in India.
- Lenders have transferred the entire Rs 9,234-crore Jaypee Infratech loan to newly constituted National Asset Reconstruction Company (NARCL). This is the

maiden acquisition by the government-promoted bad loan bank that was set a year ago. Under the arrangement, the NARCL will only acquire Jaypee Infratech loans that are currently held by 9 public sector banks.

- Microsoft announced a new multiyear, multibilliondollar investment with ChatGPT-maker OpenAI. Microsoft Corp. will be making a $10 billion worth investment in OpenAI, the research lab behind the famous ChatGPT and DALL-E. The deal marks the third phase of the partnership between the two companies, following Microsoft's previous investments in 2019 and 2021. Microsoft said the renewed partnership will accelerate breakthroughs in AI and help both companies commercialize advanced technologies in the future.

- Coal India Ltd (CIL) has envisaged processing the overburdened rocks for sand production in mines where fragmented rock or Overburden (OB) material contains about 60 percent sandstone by volume which is harnessed through crushing and processing of Overburden. During Opencast mining, the overlying soil and rocks are removed as waste to extract coal and OB is heaped in dumps.

International Current Affairs

- India and Pakistan exchanged lists of nuclear installations that cannot be attacked in the event of hostilities, maintaining a tradition dating back to 1992 despite bilateral ties being at an all-time low. The two sides further exchanged lists of prisoners held in each other's jails, and the Indian side sought the early release and repatriation of civilian prisoners, missing defence personnel and fishermen, along with their boats, from Pakistan's custody.

- Luiz Inacio Lula da Silva took office for a third term as Brazil's president, vowing to fight for the poor and the environment and "rebuild the country" after far-right leader Jair Bolsonaro's divisive administration. The 77-year-old veteran leftist, who previously led Brazil from 2003 to 2010, took the oath of office before Congress, capping a remarkable political comeback for the metalworker-turned-president less than five years after he was jailed on controversial, since-quashed corruption charges.

- The 10th edition of Dhaka Lit Fest (DLF), the largest international literary festival in Bangladesh, which was postponed three years in a row owing to the Covid-19 pandemic, is scheduled for January 5-8, 2023. The Bangla Academy in Dhaka's historic grounds will serve as the venue for the event.

- China has appointed Qin Gang, its ambassador to the United States and a trusted aide of President Xi Jinping to be its new foreign minister, as Beijing and Washington seek to stabilize rocky relations. This decision was made by the 13th National People's Congress (NPC) Standing Committee. Qin, 56, replaces Wang Yi, who has been foreign minister for the past decade.

- China's CRRC Corporation Ltd. Launched a hydrogen urban train, and it is the first in Asia and the second such train in the world. Germany introduced green trains a few months back. The hydrogen trains have a speed of 160 km per hour and the operational range without refueling is 600 km. The trains launched by Germany have a record of 1175 km range set. The Indian Railway on the other hand is moving fast to induct the 'World's Greenest Train' soon.

- The Indian government has proclaimed that they have identified two lithium mines and one copper mine in Argentina, and they are moving forward to acquiring it or taking long term lease. The government of India said that they had sent a team of geologists to Argentina to assess and find potential lithium deposits in the month of November 2022. They have been able to identify a possible source of lithium and copper deposits in the south American country.

- New satellite imagery reveals the effect of Europe's 'winter heatwave' in the thick of the continent's winter skiing season. An image posted by the European Union's Copernicus Programme shows a distinct lack of snow surrounding the Swiss town of Altdorf, which is close to skiing resorts. In Altdorf, the temperature reached 66.5°F(19.2°C) on New Year's Day and did not fall below 60.9°F(16.1°C) during the night, breaking a previous record set in 1864. Warsaw in Poland also hit 66°F(18.9°C), smashing its own January record by over 9°F(5°C).

- US has approved the first-ever vaccine for honey bees which will confer protection from the American foulbrood disease, raising hopes of a new weapon against diseases that routinely ravage colonies that are relied upon for food pollination. The US Department of Agriculture (USDA) has permitted a conditional license for a vaccine, developed by Dalan Animal Health, a US-based biotech company. The vaccine will be supplied on a "limited basis" to commercial beekeepers in the US and is expected to be available this year.

- Taiwanese lawmakers have passed new rules that let local chip firms turn 25% of their annual research and development expenses into tax credits, part of efforts to keep cutting-edge semiconductor technologies at home and maintain the island's technology leadership. Officials there have repeatedly said they will ensure the latest chip technologies remain in Taiwan, a point that has been reaffirmed by executives at Taiwan Semiconductor Manufacturing Co. and other local chip giants.

- The United States Parliament has elected Kevin McCarthy of the Republican Party as the speaker of the House of Representatives after 15 rounds of voting. He is the 55th speaker of the US House of Representatives. He was serving as the House Minority Leader in the House. He has replaced Nancy Pelosi, the leader of the Democratic Party in the House of Representatives.

- Indian-origin Sikh woman, Manpreet Monica Singh became the first ever female Sikh judge in the US after she was sworn in as a Harris County judge. Born and brought up in Houston, after her father immigrated to the US early in the 1970s, Singh currently lives in Bellaire with her husband and two children. In her career expanding over two decades, the newly appointed judge has been involved in numerous civil rights organizations at the local, state, and national levels.

- After a brief pause, Hawaii's Kilauea volcano erupted again, spewing lava fountains and discharges of volcanic ash into the air. The eruption started January 5, 2022 afternoon at the volcano's crater, according to a notice issued by the United States Geological Service (GSGS). lava from the volcano is contained in Kilauea's crater, a closed section of Hawaii Volcanoes National Park.

- Gabon's President Ali Bongo appointed the country's first female Prime Minister Rose Christiane Ossouka Raponda to the role of Vice-President and named a new PM to replace her. Former Minister Alain-Claude Bilie By Nze will replace Ossouka Raponda and form a new government, Bongo's secretary general Jean-Yves Teale said in a video statement posted on the presidency's Twitter account.

- Now Punjabi is all set to be taught in public schools in Western Australia. The language is all set to be introduced into the school curriculum. The Australian government is adopting Punjabi as the newest language after a 2021 census showed that it was the fastestgrowing language in Australia with more than

239,000 people using it at home, an increase of over 80 per cent from 2016, reported SBS Punjabi.

- The United States announced that it will extend COVID19 pandemic-era restrictions, known as Title 42, to expel migrants from Nicaragua, Cuba and Haiti caught crossing the U.S.-Mexico border back to Mexico. The move would block more nationalities from seeking asylum in the United States, and raises questions about the implications of this policy expansion and its legality. At the same time, the White House said it would open more legal pathways for migrants from those nations to apply to enter the country from abroad.

- In a rare announcement, the United States said its ballistic missile submarine, USS West Virginia, visited its Indian Ocean military base at Diego Garcia. Before it visited the base at Diego Garcia, the submarine had surfaced in the Arabian Sea and participated in a joint, US Strategic Command-directed communications exercise to validate emerging and innovative tactics in the Indian Ocean.

- Brazil's President-elect Luiz Inacio Lula da Silva announced Sonia Guajajara as the first minister of the new Ministry of Indigenous People with a mandate to oversee policies ranging from land demarcation to health care. Sonia Guajajara is widely known as the leader of the main group of Brazil's indigenous tribes and is a member of the Amazon Guajajara. She was also featured in Time Magazine's annual list of the world's 100 most influential people.

- The United Arab Emirates has named a veteran technocrat who both leads Abu Dhabi's state-run oil company and oversees its renewable energy efforts to preside over the upcoming United Nations climate negotiations in Dubai. Emirati authorities nominated Sultan al-Jaber, a confidant of UAE President Sheikh Mohammed bin Zayed Al Nahyan, who serves as CEO of the Abu Dhabi National Oil Co.

- European officials and Swedish King Carl XVI Gustaf inaugurated the EU's first mainland orbital launch complex. The European Union wants to bolster its capacity to launch small satellites into space with a new launchpad in Arctic Sweden. The new facility at Esrange Space Centre near the city of Kiruna should complement the EU's current launching capabilities in French Guiana. China's population fell last year for the first time in six decades, a historic turn that is expected to mark the start of a long period of decline in its citizen numbers with profound implications for its economy. The drop, the worst since the Great Famine of 1961, also lends weight to predictions that India will become the world's most populous nation in this year. Long-term, UN experts see China's population shrinking by 109 million by 2050, more than triple the decline of their previous forecast in 2019.

- The United Nations Security Council (UNSC) has listed Pakistan-based terrorist Abdul Rehman Makki as a global terrorist. Makki is the brother-in-law of Lashkar-e-Taiba (LeT) chief and 26/11 mastermind Hafiz Saeed. The development comes after India last year slammed China after it blocked the proposal to list Makki under the Sanctions Committee. Makki, who has been involved in raising funds, recruiting, and radicalizing the youth to plan attacks in India, especially in Jammu and Kashmir, has already been listed as a terrorist by India and the United States.

- India will support Sri Lanka's debt restructuring plan as the island nation looks to trim its huge public expenditure to win approval for a crucial bailout from the International Monetary Fund. India formally notified that it would support Sri Lanka's debt restructuring plan. New Delhi's backing comes at a critical time for Sri Lanka as it has to put its massively indebted public finances in order to unlock a $2.9 billion IMF loan that was agreed in September. The IMF has stressed the importance of joint talks involving three of Sri Lanka's main bilateral creditors - China, Japan and India.

- India has announced donation of 12,500 doses of pentavalent vaccines to Cuba. Minister of State for External Affairs Meenakshi Lekhi announced this during her official visit to Cuba. This was her first visit to Cuba. Pentavalent vaccine provides protection to a child from 5 life-threatening diseases -Diphtheria, Pertussis, Tetanus, Hepatitis B and HIV.

- The United Nations General Assembly(UNGA) adopted a resolution titled 'Education for Democracy' that reaffirms the right of everyone to education. The resolution, which was co-sponsored by India, recognises that "education for all" contributes to the strengthening of democracy. The resolution encourages member states to integrate education for democracy into their education standards.

- Aruna Miller has scripted history by becoming the first Indian-American politician to be sworn in as the Lieutenant Governor in the state of Maryland, adjoining the US capital. Aruna, 58, a former delegate to the Maryland House, made history when the Democrat became the 10th Lieutenant Governor of the state.

- FITUR is the global meeting point for tourism professionals and the leading trade fair for inbound and outbound markets in Latin America. FITUR is the second most important tourism fair in the world. Around 10,000 national and international companies take part in each edition and there are more than 50,000 visitors spread over the different days of the event. The fair is being organized in Madrid, Spain.

- A 30-year-old Indian-American attorney, Janani Ramachandran has emerged as the youngest and the first queer woman of colour to take oath as the Oakland City Council member in the U.S. state of California. She took the ceremonial oath wearing a saree as the Oakland City Council member for District 4 in an inauguration ceremony.

- The continuous anti-corruption campaign has prompted President Nguyen Xuan Phuc of Vietnam to announce his resignation. In Vietnam, the anti-corruption campaign has resulted in the dismissal of several ministers. Two of President Phuc's deputy prime ministers had resigned earlier.

- The United Arab Emirates is in early discussions with India to trade non-oil commodities in Indian rupees, Minister for Foreign Trade Dr Thani Al Zeyoudi said in World Economic Forum, Davos. The minister said other countries, including China, had also raised the issue of settling non-oil trade payments in local currencies. He added that the UAE is hoping to conclude a trade agreement with Cambodia in the first quarter.

- External Affairs Minister S. Jaishankar has extended a concessional USD 40 million Line of Credit for developing sporting infrastructure in the Maldives. It is a part of New Delhi's efforts to bring Prime Minister Narendra Modi's flagship projects such as fit India and Khelo India into the stretch of the Neighborhood First Policy. External Affairs Minister S. Jaishankar is on a visit to the Maldives to further expand bilateral engagement with the key maritime neighbor of India.

- New Zealand's former COVID-19 response minister, Chris Hipkins will replace Jacinda Ardern as prime minister. The 44-year-old senior politician must be formally backed by Labour members of parliament to take over as the country's 41st prime minister, following Ardern's shock resignation. As leader of the governing party, Hipkins will also become prime minister when Ardern steps down.

- Brazil and Argentina aim for greater economic integration, including the development of a common currency, Brazilian President Luiz Inacio Lula da Silva and Argentine leader Alberto Fernandez said in a joint article they penned. They also decided to advance discussions on a common South American currency that can be used for both financial and commercial flows, reducing costs of operations and external vulnerability.

- Brazil's ministry of health has declared a medical emergency in the Yanomami territory, the country's largest indigenous reservation bordering Venezuela, following reports of children dying of malnutrition and other diseases caused by illegal gold mining.

- World's longest calligraphic mural Makkah: The Grand Mosque Road in Makkah now features the longest calligraphic painting in the world, the most recent addition to the holy city's aesthetic appeal. The 75metre mural, created by the artist Amal Felemban, is one of a number of sculptures and installations that already beautify Makkah as part of a programme conducted by the local government to improve its aesthetic appeal and show off Saudi heritage and culture to pilgrims.

- The White House nominated a special envoy for human rights in North Korea, moving to fill a post that has been empty since 2017 amid debate over how rights issues fit with efforts to counter Pyongyang's nuclear weapons programme. President Joe Biden nominated Julie Turner, a long-time diplomat and current director of the Office of East Asia and the Pacific in the Bureau of Democracy, Human Rights and Labor at the Department of State.

- China is constructing a new dam on the Mabja Zangbo river, geospatial intelligence researcher Damien Symon has claimed. The dam will be sitting just a few kilometres north of the Indian-Nepali-Chinese border trijunction. Satellite images show work is being done on the Mabja Zangbo river in Tibet's Burang County since 2021. While the construction of the dam is not complete, it does pose questions regarding China's hegemony on water supplies downstream in the future.

- Canadian Prime Minister Justin Trudeau has announced a new federal investment to build and commercialise the world's first photonic based, faulttolerant quantum computer. The quantum computer will have the potential to provide world leading capabilities to help solve complex data problems and could be used in a variety of sectors such as finance, transportation, environmental modelling and health.

- A US Military raid in Somalia killed a key regional leader of the Islamic State group, Bilal al-Sudani. The US Military raid was ordered by President Joe Biden. Bilal al Sudani was killed during a gunfight after US troops descended on a mountainous cave complex in northern Somalia hoping to capture him. Around 10 of Sudani's Islamic State associates at the scene were killed, but there were no American casualties.

- Indian American astronaut Raja Chari was nominated by US President Joe Biden for the post of Air Force brigadier general. The nomination has yet to be confirmed by the US Senate. The senate approves all senior civilian and military appointments, according to the US Defense Department. Brigadier General (BG) is a one-star General Officer rank of the United States Air Force.

- Petr Pavel, a former chairman of the North Atlantic Treaty Organisation (NATO) military committee, has become the new president of the Czech Republic. Pavel, 61, defeated billionaire Andrej Babis in a run-off vote to replace controversial President Milos Zeman as he emerged as the new Czech President. A former military general, Pavel got more than 58 per cent of the vote, according to the Czech Statistics Office.

National Current Affairs

- Union Home and Cooperation Minister Shri Amit Shah has laid the foundation stone of the Central Detective Training Institute (CDTI) at Devanahalli in Karnataka and inaugurated the residential and administrative complexes of the Indo-Tibetan Border Police (ITBP). The residential complexes of ITBP inaugurated by Shri Amit Shah include Residential Quarters, Joint Building, Barracks for 120 Jawans, Staff Officers' Mess and Officers' Mess.

- The National Commission for Indian System of Medicine (NCISM) and the Central Council for Research in Ayurvedic Sciences (CCRAS), the two prominent institutions under the Ministry of Ayush, Government of India for regulating medical education and conducting scientific research respectively, have launched

'SMART' (Scope for Mainstreaming Ayurveda Research in Teaching Professionals). The program aimed to boost scientific research in priority healthcare research areas through Ayurveda colleges and hospitals. A five-judge Constitution Bench of the Supreme Court upheld the Modi government's 2016 decision to demonetise Rs 500 and Rs 1,000 currency notes, saying the decision was about executive policy and could not be reversed. The court rejected the 58 petitions challenging demonetisation and said the decisionmaking process of the government was not flawed.

- Prime Minister Narendra Modi inaugurated the Dr. Syama Prasad Mookerjee National Institute of Water and Sanitation (SPM-NIWAS) at Joka in Kolkata via video conferencing. SPM-NIWAS has been set up with a budget of Rs 100 crore, on 8.72 acres of land at Joka, Diamond Harbour Road, Kolkata, West Bengal.

- The Government of India is proposing the ban on promotion of Online Betting on the Social Media platforms. The Information Technology (Intermediary Guidelines and Digital Media Ethics Code) Rules, 2021 have recently been recommended for revision by the Central government to control the Indian online gaming market. The suggestion was made to protect consumers from any harm that skill-based games might cause.

- The President of India Droupadi Murmu inaugurated Samvidhan Udyan, Mayur Stambh, National Flag Post, Statue of Mahatma Gandhi, and Maharana Pratap at Raj Bhavan, Jaipur on 3rd January 2023. The President of India virtually inaugurated the Transmission System for Solar Energy Zones in Rajasthan and laid the foundation stone for the 1000 MV Bikaner Solar Power Project of SJVN Limited.

- In a draft change of IT rules, the government proposes self-regulatory organizations for international online gaming companies operating in India, but it will not permit betting. The draft online gaming guidelines released on Monday included steps to protect consumers from the risk of gaming addiction and financial loss as well as user authentication.

- Prime Minister Narendra Modi to launch the world's longest river cruise, "Ganga Vilas" from Varanasi, Uttar Pradesh to Dibrugarh, Assam on 13th January 2023. Chief Minister Yogi Adityanath has informed us that all preparations for the arrival of the Prime Minister and the launch ceremony in Varanasi should be finished.

- The President of India Droupadi Murmu inaugurated the 18th National Jamboree of the Bharat Scouts and Guides at Pali, Rajasthan on 4th January 2023. The President of India noted that the Bharat Scouts and Guides is the largest voluntary, non-political, uniformed youth organization and educational movement in the country. India has taken over the leadership of the Asia Pacific Postal Union (APPU) in January 2023. Dr Vinaya Prakash Singh will take over the charge of Secretary General of the Union for a tenure of 4 years. This is the result of the elections during the 13th APPU Congress held in August-September 2022.

- Silent Valley National Park in the last month identified 141 species of birds of which 17 were new species of birds. A total of 175 species of birds have been spotted in Silent Valley. The bird survey was conducted at Silent Valley on the 27th, 28th, and 29th of December 2022 and marked the 30th Anniversary of the first bird survey in Silent Valley. The bird survey was first conducted in the last week of December 1990, however, due to Covid-19, the anniversary could not be celebrated in December 2020.

- Union Minister of Agriculture and Farmers' Welfare Narendra Singh Tomar inaugurated the three-day 'Northeast Krishi Kumbhar-2023' and took part in the 49th Foundation Day celebration of the ICAR Research Complex for NEH Region, Umiam. The Minister inaugurated the administrative cum academic block office and Girl's Hostel of the College of Agriculture at Kyrdemkulai, Ri Bhoi district.

- President Droupadi Murmu laid the foundation stone of state-owned energy firm SJVN's 1,000 MV Bikaner Solar Power Project. The event was done virtually by the President of India in Jaipur, Rajasthan. The project is being implemented by SJVN Limited through its owned subsidiary SJVN Green Energy Limited (SGEL).

- Union Health and Family Welfare and Chemicals and Fertilizers Minister Dr. Mansukh Mandaviya announced that India's first-ever coal gasification-based Talcher Fertilizer Plant in Odisha will be ready to be dedicated to the nation by October 2024. Union Minister Mansukh Mandaviya visited the site on the second day and noted that the work in the plant in Talcher is in progress.

- Prime Minister has launched the government's Aspirational Block Programme (ABP), which is aimed at improving the performance of blocks lagging on various development parameters. The Aspirational Blocks Programme is on the lines of the Aspirational District Programme that was launched in 2018 and covers 112 districts across the country.

- Union Home Minister Amit Shah inaugurated a 120-foottall statue of a polo player riding a polo at Marjing Polo Complex in Imphal, Manipur. Manipur is known as the birthplace of the game polo. Chief Minister of Manipur N Biren Singh was also present during the inauguration ceremony and gave a polo mallet and a painting of the game to Home Minister Amit Shah.

- Union Minister of State Science and Technology, Dr. Jitendra Singh released the theme for the "National Science Day 2023", titled "Global Science for Global Wellbeing" at National Media Centre. National Science Day is celebrated in India on 28th February every year to mark the discovery of the Raman Effect by Indian physicist CV Raman on 28th February 1928.

- The 28th edition of Saarang, India's largest student-run festival begins at IIT Madras. Saarang 2023 will feature more than 100 events with participation from 500 colleges across the country. It is expected to see over 80,000 people at the festival. The fest will be held till 15th January 2023. The theme of this year's Saarang edition is 'Mystic Hues'.

- Union Home Minister Amit Shah inaugurated the 'Jai Hindi' Light and Sound Show at Red Fort, in New Delhi. The show will include a Mathrubhumi Show, in which India's history of thousands of years has been integrated. The show will be for one hour and it is divided into three parts. It will highlight the rise of the Marathas, the war of Independence in 1857, the rise of the Indian National Army and INA trials, and the fight for Independence.

- Union Minister Sarbananda Sonowal, along with Tripura Chief Minister Dr. Manik Saha, inaugurated the School of Logistics, Waterways and Communication in Agartala. This new institution aims to provide world-class education and training to the region's talented individuals, allowing them to excel in the transportation and logistics industry.

- The world's longest river cruise, the MV Ganga Vilas, which will travel 3,200 km over 27 river systems in five states in India and Bangladesh in 51 days, was launched by Prime Minister Narendra Modi on Friday, January 13, 2022. The 51-

day cruise has 50 stops planned, including major cities like Patna in Bihar, Sahibganj in Jharkhand, Kolkata in West Bengal, Dhaka in Bangladesh, and Guwahati in Assam. These destinations include world heritage sites, national parks, river ghats, and world heritage sites.

- The Ministry of Culture has organized a grand curtain raiser cultural program 'Sur Sarita'-Symphony of Ganga' on the launch event of the world's longest river cruise at Varanasi. Prime Minister Narendra Modi flagged off the cruise on 13th January 2023. The grand concert named 'Sur Sarita'-Symphony of Ganga' was led by the renowned Indian singer Shankar Mahadevan at Kashi Vishwanath Corridor.

- Digital India Startup Hub, through the Software Technology Parks of India, shall set up India's first Centre of Excellence in Online Gaming at Shillong by March 2023. This was announced by Minister of State for Electronics & Information Technology and Skill Development & Entrepreneurship, Rajeev Chandrasekhar, at a function in Meghalaya's capital.

- Prime Minister Narendra Modi will virtually flag off the semi-high speed train Vande Bharat Express from Secunderabad Railway Station on January 15 as a gift to the Telugu people on the occasion of Sankranti. Union Minister of Railways Ashwini Vaishnaw and Union Culture Minister G Kishan Reddy will be physically present at Secunderabad Railway Station. The Vande Bharat Train will run between Secunderabad and Visakhapatnam in approximately eight hours.

- This year, SPIC MACAY, in association with the Ministry of Culture and the New Delhi Municipal Council, presents "Shruti Amrut," a new instalment of its wildly popular "Music in the Park" series. Eminent musicians from all over the nation performed to highlight the beauty of Indian classical music.

- Prime Minister Narendra Modi shared snippets titled "Your Exam, Your Methods-Choose Your Own Style" from the Exam Warriors Book and has urged students to share how they prepare for exams. PM Modi in his message shared that in the book Exam Warriors, one mantra is "Your Exam, Your Methods-Choose Your Own Style".

- The National Council for Education Research and Training (NCERT) has released India's first national assessment regulator, PARAKH, which will work on setting norms, standards, and guidelines for student assessment and evaluation for all recognized school boards in the country. The PARAKH regulator aims to set up assessment guidelines for all boards to help remove disparities in the scores of students enrolled with different state boards. PARAKH stands for The Performance Assessment, Review, and Analysis of Knowledge for Holistic Development.

- Prime Minister Narendra Modi inaugurated the second phase of Saansad Khel Mahakumbh 2022-23 via video conferencing. Saansad Khel Mahakumbh 2022-23 has been organized in Basti district, Uttar Pradesh by Harish Dwivedi, Member of Parliament from Basti since 2021.

- The Indian Olympic Association (IOA) formed a seven-member committee, including M C Mary Kom and Yogeshwar Dutt, to probe the allegations of sexual harassment against Wrestling Federation of India president Brij Bhushan Sharan Singh by top grapplers. This comes after the agitating wrestlers had earlier in the day reached out to the IOA, demanding formation of an enquiry committee to probe the allegations against Singh, a day after threatening to lodge multiple FIRs against the WFI chief.

- "Nari Shakti" (women power) will be driving the theme of this year's Republic Day tableau of Navy. Not just the front of the tableau will feature a woman aircrew of a Dornier aircraft flying overhead, but Lt. Commander Disha Amrith has been tasked with commanding its parade contingent.

- After the success of the Co-WIN platform, the government has now replicated it to set up an electronic registry for routine vaccinations. Named U-WIN, the programme to digitise India's Universal Immunisation Programme (UIP) has been launched in a pilot mode in two districts of each state and Union Territory. Carrying vaccination cards of children and pregnant women, struggling to keep a tab on the next jab and other such hassles may soon become a thing of the past.

- The Indian Railways has successfully concluded the trial of an Artificial Intelligence Programme it built to fix the endless problem of the Waiting list. The Indian Railways has also introduced the Ideal Train Profile to maximize the capacity utilization and revenue generation in reserved mail express trains by regularly analyzing the demand pattern of every single train.

- South Africa said that it had reached a deal to transfer more than 100 cheetahs to India as part of an ambitious project to reintroduce the spotted cats in the south Asian country. The environment ministry said an initial batch of 12 cheetahs would be flown to India next month, after eight cheetahs arrived from Namibia last September.

- The six-day mega event "Bharat Parv" Event is to be organized by the Government of India at the Lawns and Gyan Path in front of Red Fort, Delhi from 26th to 31st January 2023, as part of the Republic Day Celebrations. "Bharat Parv" is under the Ministry of Tourism and has been designated as the nodal Ministry for the event.

- Over 11 Crore rural households in the country have access to tap water connections as India celebrates its 74th Republic Day. 123 districts and more than 1.53 lakh villages of India have reported 'Har Ghar Jal' which means every household has access to clean drinking water through the tap. Jal Jeevan Mission was announced by Prime Minister Narendra Modi on 15th August 2019 to provide every rural household with a tap water connection by 2024.

- PepsiCo Foundation, the philanthropic arm of PepsiCo and CARE, have launched 'She Feeds the World' program in India to strengthen the role of small-scale women producers through sustainable training and economic support. The program, which will be implemented in the Alipurduar and Cooch Behar districts of West Bengal, aims to reach out to more than 48,000 women, men and children and indirectly benefit 1,50,000 individuals.

- The biennial air show and aviation expo, Aero India 2023, is scheduled for February 13-17. Yelahanka Air Force Station in Bengaluru, which has hosted it since 1996, will serve as the venue. Prime Minister Narendra Modi will inaugurate the programme. More than 730 exhibitors from India and other countries will take part in the event this year.

- The Mughal Garden of Rashtrapati Bhavan has been called Amrit Udyan. As President Droupadi Murmu on Sunday inaugurated Udyan Utsav-2023, the opening of the Rashtrapati Bhavan grounds, the renowned park is expected to open to the public on January 31.

- The Indian Council of Historical Research (ICHR) organized an exhibition on Medieval Indian Dynasties by a division of the Union Ministry of Education and featured 50 different dynasties in the exhibitions. In the exhibition of the Indian Council of Historical Research no Muslim dynasty was displayed.

- Minister for Ports, Shipping and Waterways Sarbananda Sonowal inaugurated the National Logistics Portal (marine) in New Delhi. It is a one-stop platform aimed at connecting all the stakeholders of the logistics community using IT. The National Logistic Portal (marine) (NLP) is a project of national importance. This will improve efficiency and transparency by reducing costs and promote the growth of the logistics sector.

States Current Affairs

- Kerala Chief Minister Pinarayi Vijayan inaugurated Indian Library Congress in Kannur, Kerala. The inauguration event of the Indian Library Congress was organized by the People's Mission for Social Development and Library Council.

- Himachal Pradesh Chief Minister Sukhvinder Singh Sukhu announced to set up of Rs 101 crore CM's Sukhashraya Sahayata Kosh for the destitute in the state. Chief Minister of Himachal Pradesh informed that 40 Congress MLAs agreed to contribute Rs one lakh each from their first salary for the fund and also requested the MLAs from BJP and other parties to contribute.

- India's first green hydrogen blending operation in the piped natural gas (PNG) network at NTPC Kawas, Gujarat. The project is a joint effort of NTPC and Gujarat Gas (GCL). The power generation company stated that the first molecular of green hydrogen from the project was set in motion by P Ram Prasad, Head of Project, Kawas in presence of other senior executives of NTPC Kawas and GCL. After the start of blending and operation, NTPC Kawas held an awareness workshop for township residents with help of GCL officials. The foundation stone of the project was laid by the Prime Minister of India, Narendra Modi on 30th July 2022.

- Defence minister Rajnath Singh has inaugurated the Siyom bridge in Arunachal Pradesh, along with 27 other infrastructure projects completed by the Border Roads Organisation (BRO). Built at a cost of 724 crore rupees, these projects will hugely augment India's border infrastructure, mostly along the Chinese border, from Ladakh to Arunachal.

- The Gaan Ngai of the Zeliangrong Community celebrated in Manipur. The Gaan Ngai festival is one of the major festivals of Manipur which is celebrated every year after harvesting. The festival also marks the end of the year when the farmers have stored their foodgrains in their granaries. During the festival, the Zeliangrong Community shows their gratitude by offering the Almighty a good harvest and praying for a better and prosperous life in the coming year.

- Imoinu Day is celebrated in Manipur as a part of the Meitei Cultural ritual. The traditional festival of Imoinu Day is celebrated on the 12th day of the Meitei Lunar Month of Wakching. Every year on this day, people of the valley serve dishes in odd numbers as part of the Imoinu Eratpa ritual. They regard Imoinu Eratpa as a goddess of health, prosperity, abundance, and order of domesticity in Manipur.

- The Union Cabinet has approved the naming of Greenfield International Airport at Goa's Mopa as Manohar International Airport after former Defence Minister and Goa Chief Minister Manohar Parrikar. The airport was inaugurated by Prime Minister Narendra Modi in December 2022 at Mopa Goa. The airport will be named after the late Manohar Parrikar to honor his contribution to building modern Goa.

- West Bengal Chief Minister Mamata Banerjee launched a new campaign "Didi'r Surakha Kavach" for her party, Trinamool Congress. The campaign "Didi'r Surakha Kavach" ahead of the panchayat polls due in April. The "Didi'r Surakha Kavach" will begin on 10th January 2023.

- Chief Minister Shivraj Singh Chouhan launched the Madhya Pradesh Residential Land Rights scheme (Mukhyamantri Awasiya Bhu Adhikar Yojana) to distribute free leases of residential land to selected beneficiaries. The scheme aims to provide free plots to the poor living in rural areas for building their houses. The land will be offered completely free of cost and along with the plot, the benefits of all other schemes will also be delivered.

- Kerala Chief Minister (CM) Pinarayi Vijayan has inaugurated the Palm leaf Manuscript Museum with modern audio-visual technology at the renovated Central Archives, Fort area in Thiruvananthapuram, Kerala. The Museum promoted as

"World's First PalmLeaf Manuscript Museum" was set up by the Archives Department in association with the Kerala Museum of History and Heritage at a cost of Rs 3 crore.

- Octave 2023 is a festival being held under the aegis of the South Zone Culture Centre, Thanjavur, Tamil Nadu to showcase the indigenous art and culture of Northeast India. Octave 2023 was inaugurated by Tamil Nadu Governor R N Ravi.
- The eagerly anticipated Purple Fest, Celebrating Diversity, the state's first-ever inclusive festival for people with disabilities (PwDs), will take place in Goa. Panjim will host the festival from January 6-8, 2023, with all the fanfare.
- Mysuru and Hampi are the two popular destinations in Karnataka to be promoted as a part of the new Tourism policy 'The Swadesh Darshan 2.0 Scheme, which focuses on revving up destination tourism. Mysuru and Hampi are among the 19 places identified across the eight states and UTs in India to be promoted under the Swadesh Darshan 2.0 Scheme.
- Chief Minister Pinarayi Vijayan declared Kerala as the first state in the country to go fully digital in its banking service and said this recognition would boost the state economy. Vijayan said this achievement was possible due to social interventions through local selfgovernment institutions along with infrastructure development and technological advances in the banking sector.
- The Kerala Cabinet approved a scheme to ensure those employed under the Mahatma Gandhi Rural Employment Guarantee Scheme (MGNREGS) in the poll-bound state get benefits like pension and medical assistance. It has been recommended that governor Arif Mohammad Khan issue an ordinance in this regard. With this, Kerala became the first state to have a welfare board for the beneficiaries of employment guarantee programmes in the country. At least 26.71 lakh labourers under the Mahatma Gandhi National Rural Employment Guarantee programme and 2.5 lakh workers of the Ayyankali Urban Employment Guarantee Scheme will receive the benefits of the newly formed welfare board.
- Chhattisgarh Chief Minister Bhupesh Baghel celebrated the Cherchera festival at Dudhadhari Math in Raipur, Chhattisgarh. The Cherchera festival of Chhattisgarh is celebrated on the full moon night of the 'Paush' Hindu calendar month. It is to celebrate the happiness and joy of taking crops to their homes after cultivation.

Chief Minister Baghel extended warm wishes to all the citizens of Chhattisgarh on the auspicious occasion.

- Kerala's 'Year of Enterprises' Project was recognized as the best practices model at the National Conference on Micro Small and Medium Enterprises chaired by Prime Minister Narendra Modi. The Project aimed to create 1,00,000 enterprises and has successfully created 1,18,509 enterprises and got investment worth ₹7,261.54 crores.

- Uttarakhand Governor Lt Gen Gurmit Singh (retd) has approved the 30 percent horizontal reservation to domicile women of the state in the government jobs bill. The state assembly of Uttarakhand passed the Uttarakhand Public Services (Horizontal Reservation for women) Bill on 29th November 2022. The beneficiaries need to be women with a domicile certificate of Uttarakhand.

- The Indian High Commission signed an MoU with the Sabaragamuwa University of Sri Lanka to establish a Hindi Chair. The MoU aims to establish the Hindi Chair as a part of India's cultural connection through the Indian Council for Cultural Relations. The Indian Mission will also award a gold medal to the best-performing student of the Hindi Chair. The Sabaragamuwa University is a public university located in Belihuloya, Balangoda, Sri Lanka.

- Kerala has kicked itself into the Guinness Book of World Records by taking 4,500 penalty kicks in 12 hours. The Department of Sports and Youth Affairs made it possible for the football-crazy State to set the Guinness record at a Dream Goal penalty shootout organised at Payyanad Football Stadium at Manjeri.

- Mongeet is a festival of music, poetry, art, craft, food, culinary techniques, indigenous herbs, and culture celebrated in Majuli, Assam. The Mongeet festival started in the year 2020 as a movement of arts and music and it aims to nurture the upcoming musical talents of Assam.

- The 'Saharsh' was launched in 40 schools of the state on a pilot basis in August last year. This year, it will be extended to all government and aided schools in Tripura from the second week of January.

- The renowned Jallikattu bull-taming competition got underway in the Tamil Nadu village of Avaniyapuram. Aneesh Sekhar, the district collector of Madurai, as saying that preparations had been made to ensure a successful Jallikattu. ensuring the players' and bulls' safety. Bulls are protected in the play area by three levels of barricading, as are spectators.

- The Himachal Pradesh government restored the old pension scheme in its first cabinet meeting. The cabinet decided to provide OPS to all government employees who are presently covered under the defined contributory pension scheme, also referred to as NPS. This scheme will benefit about 1.36 lakh NPS employees in the state.

- Uttar Pradesh (UP) has emerged as the top location for mobile gamers, followed by Maharashtra, Rajasthan, Bihar, and West Bengal, according to the India Mobile Gaming Report 2022 issued by the gaming platform Mobile Premier League (MPL).

- The Indian district of Kollam has become the country's first constitution literate district. The announcement was made by Kerala Chief Minister Pinarayi Vijayan. The district's success is the result of a seven-month campaign launched by the Kollam district panchayat, District Planning Committee, and the Kerala Institute of Local Administration (KILA) to educate citizens about the country's laws and their rights.

- National Hydroelectric Power Corporation (NHPC) has submitted a pre-feasibility report to the Central Electricity Authority of India for the 'Upper Siang Multipurpose Storage', India's largest hydel power project to date to come up in Arunachal Pradesh. This will be the 11-Gigawatt (GW) project. India may spend ₹1.13 trillion to build the Upper Siang multi-purpose storage project at Yingkiong in Arunachal Pradesh.

- A rare, orange-colored bat was spotted in the Banana plantation in Parali Bodal village of Kanger Valley National Park in Bastar, Chhattisgarh. The orangecolored bat is identified as a 'Painted Bat' and is characterized by bright orange and black wings.

- Higher Education Minister in Kerala R Bindu announced that girls students above the age of 18 years will get maternity leave of 60 days. The required attendance percentage for female students will be 73 percent including menstrual leave. The attendance percentage required earlier was 75 percent.

- Kerala's Wayanad becomes the first district in the country to provide basic documents and facilities such as Aadhaar cards, ration cards, birth/death certificates, election ID cards, bank accounts and health insurance to all tribespeople.

- Chief Minister of Odisha, Naveen Patnaik inaugurated an 'International Craft Summit' in Jajpur. The International Craft Summit is the first-of-its-kind craft summit to feature pioneer craftspersons, culture, and art enthusiasts. CM Naveen Patnaik addressed the inaugural event of the International Craft Summit virtually and noted that it is a historic occasion for Odisha.

- Punjab Chief Minister Bhagwant Mann launched the 'School of Eminence', an ambitious project of the Punjab government. CM Bhagwant Mann noted that it is a revolutionary step towards ensuring a bright future for students. The Punjab government fixed a budget of Rs 200 crore for the 'School of Eminence' project.

- Assam Chief Minister Himanta Biswa Sarma announced that the Centre has nominated the maidams of Ahom Kingdom in Charaideo to seek a UNESCO World Heritage Site tag. The historic maidams of Ahom Kingdom in Charaideo were chosen out of 52 sites for the UNESCO World Heritage Site tag.

- Union Home Minister Amit Shah awarded the Aska Police Station of Ganjam, district of Odisha as the number one police station in the country. Aska Police station was awarded in the annual ranking of Police station for 2022. Aska Police station received the prestigious award along with the certificate of appreciation from Union Minister Amit Shah.

- Himachal Pradesh celebrates its 53rd Statehood Day with joy and enthusiasm across the state on 25th January 2023. In 1971, on this day, Himachal Pradesh became the 18th state of India. The state-level function of Full Statehood Day was held at Hamirpur district, where Chief Minister Sukhwinder Singh Sukhu hoisted the national flag and took a salute from the march past presented by various contingents.

- The third edition of the two-day Orange Festival has been organized in Nagaland's Rusoma village to mark the harvest of organic oranges in the district. The orange festival was held from 24th to 25th January 2023. The orange festival is held to display the harvested oranges from the village.

- Luminous Power Technologies revealed that it has planned to build India's first green energy-based solar panel manufacturing plant in Uttarakhand which will be operational by the end of this year. The location of the new India's first green energy-based solar panel is Rudrapur which will be equipped with the latest technology to design and produce high-quality solar panels that will be used for both residential and commercial applications.

- Woxsen University has launched Project Aspirations with its firm belief in developing its ecosystem and empowering the community around the campus. Woxsen University has conceptualized the project for the ambitious girls of Classes IX-XII, Telangana Model School & Junior College. Under Project Aspiration, students are selected by the school principal to take part in the "Train the Trainer" workshop which commenced in December 2022.

- Shivraj Singh Chouhan, the chief minister of Madhya Pradesh, has made a significant statement for the women to launch the "Ladli Bahna Yojana" in the state following the success of the Ladli Laxmi Yojana for the girls. No matter their caste or status, underprivileged women would receive Rs 1,000 each month under this Yojna in order to gain financial independence.

Schemes/Committees News

- The Deendayal Antyodaya Yojana-National Rural Livelihood Mission (DAY-NRLM) has launched the Prajjwala Challenge. The Prajjwala Challenge has been launched to invite ideas, solutions, and actions that can transform rural development. It will provide a platform where ideas are invited from individuals, social enterprises, start-ups, the private sector, civil society, community-based organizations, academic institutions, incubation centers, investors, etc having the potential to transform the rural economy.

- The Union Cabinet approved an initial outlay of Rs 19,744 crore for the National Green Hydrogen Mission. Addressing the nation on its 75th Independence Day in 2021, Prime Minister Narendra Modi launched a national mission for green fuels in line with the Centre's stated target of making India energy-independent before completing 100 years of Independence. The mission will have four components that aim at enhancing domestic production of green hydrogen and promote the manufacturing of electrolysers - a key constituent for making green hydrogen.

- Prasar Bharati's broadcast infrastructure and network, the Cabinet Committee on Economic Affairs (CCEA) approved a scheme worth more than Rs 2,500 crore for Doordarshan and All India Radio. Under the scheme, eight lakh DD Free Dish DTH set top boxes (STBs) will also be distributed to people living in remote, tribal, LWE, border areas and 'aspirational' districts.

- The Ministry of Home Affairs (MHA) in India has established a High-Powered Committee (HPC) to address issues related to the protection of Ladakh's culture, language, land, and employment opportunities. A 17-member committee has been constituted under the Chairmanship of Minister of State for Home Affairs Nityanand Rai.

- PM Narendra Modi approved the new integrated food security scheme for providing free food grains to AAY and PHH beneficiaries. The new scheme has been named Pradhan Mantri Garib Kalyan Ann Yojana (PMGKAY). Under PMGKAY, free food grains will be provided, and two subsidy schemes will be included to strengthen the provision of NFSA 2013. Govt to spend 2 lakh crores for food subsidies in 2023.

- The MAARG (Mentorship, Advisory, Assistance, Resilience, and Growth) platform will be launched by Commerce and Industry Minister Piyush Goyal. The Commerce Ministry said MAARG, a portal to facilitate mentorship for start-ups across diverse sectors, and geographies, will go live on January 16.

- Prime Minister Narendra Modi announced a new 'Aarogya Maitri' project under which India will provide essential medical supplies to any developing country affected by natural disasters or humanitarian crisis and proposed to set up a 'centre of excellence' to facilitate development solutions to these countries.

- The success of "Womaniya on Government eMarketplace" was commemorated in New Delhi. The event was held by Government eMarketplace (GeM) in partnership with the self-employed women's association, Bharat (SEWA Bharat), and attended by women entrepreneurs and participants from stakeholders' organizations and associations.

- The Ministry of Minority Affairs (MoMA) has discontinued the scheme of interest subsidy on education loans for overseas studies for students belonging to minority communities (Padho Pardesh). All banks were notified by the Indian Banks' Association last month about the discontinuation of the Padho Pardesh Interest Subsidy Scheme from 2022-23. The scheme so far has been implemented through Canara Bank, the designated nodal bank.

- The Atal Pension Yojana achieved the highest-ever takers in 2022 with a rise of 36 percent in enrolment. In the Atal Pension Yojana, the figures cross the 10 million marks for the first time in a calendar year. The number of enrolments in 2022 rose to 12.5 million from 9.2 million in 2021.

- The Secretary of the Ministry of Culture Govind Mohan announced that the government is to hand over around 1,000 monuments under the control of the Archaeological Survey of India to the private sector for their upkeep under the Monument Mitra Scheme. Corporate entities will take over the monuments as part of their Corporate Social Responsibility. Under the scheme, monument amenities will be revamped by the private sector.

Agreement/Memorandum of Understanding (MoU)

- IIT Madras Centre of Excellence is working with DRDO on Advanced Defence Technologies including Combat Vehicle Technologies. Indian Institute of Technology Madras (IIT Madras) is operating a Research Centre dedicated to defence technologies jointly with the Defence Research and Development Organisation (DRDO) to develop advanced technologies for the national defence and security needs of the nation. It was established by DRDO, but IIT Madras has now taken over and converted it into a center of excellence.

- The International Hockey Federation (FIH) has signed a partnership with the JSW Group for the upcoming FIH Odisha Hockey Men's World Cup 2023 Bhubaneswar-Rourkela, which will kick-off later this month. The group supports and promotes Olympics in India and has created an Olympic Training Institute in the Inspire Institute of Sport as well as has Olympic training centres across the country. The 15th edition of FIH's flagship event for men will be played from 13 January to 29 January in Odisha, India.

- Neeru Yadav, a.k.a. "Hockey Wali Sarpanch," has launched a fresh effort to support the farmers of Lambi Ahir Village. Yadav and NABARD have signed an agreement to launch the Farmers Producers Organization (FPO) with the help of SIIRD (Society of Indian Institute of Rural Development).

- India and Panama have signed MoU to encourage cooperation in the training of diplomats. The MoU between India and Panama was signed by the External Affairs Minister of India Dr. Subramanyam Jaishankar and the Foreign Minister of Panama Janaina Tewaney Mencomon in Indore, Madhya Pradesh. The Ministers have discussed the opportunities for greater economic, health, finance, and people-to-people linkage.

- Madhya Pradesh Tourism Board signed a Memorandum of Understanding (MoU) with chapters of 8 countries of the Global Organization of People of Indian Origin (GOPIO) at the 17th Pravasi Bhartiya Divas convention. The event was held at MP Tourism Pavilion at Brilliant Convention Centre in Indore. The MoUs were signed with France Metropole Paris, Mauritius, Reunion Island, Martinique, Sri Lanka, GOPOI International, Malaysia, and Mauritius.

- Warehousing Development Regulatory Authority (WDRA) has signed a memorandum of understanding (MoU) with the State Bank of India to help farmers in getting low-interest-rate loans. The Memorandum of Understanding (MoU) was signed to promote awareness about the new loan product called 'Produce Marketing Loan' to exclusively fund against e-NWRs (electronic Negotiable Warehouse Receipt).

- Taiwan-headquartered electric vehicle and infrastructure company Gogoro is advancing its plans to deploy battery swapping network in India. The company along with Belrise Industries (formerly known as Badve Engineering) has inked a strategic energy partnership with the Maharashtra government to establish a battery swapping infrastructure. This follows Gogoro's earlier announced partnership with Hero MotoCorp and Zypp Electric among others.

- The Indian Ports Association (IPA) and Research & Information System for Developing Countries (RIS) signed a Memorandum of Agreement for setting up a Centre for Maritime Economy and Connectivity in the presence of the Minister for Ports, Shipping & Waterways and Ayush Shri Sarbananda Sonowal. During the function, various other dignitaries were also present including senior officials from MoPSW, RIS, and IPA.

- The International Hockey Federation (FIH) Partners with JSP Foundation for Hockey Development and Men's World Cup Lausanne, Switzerland. The International Hockey Federation (FIH) is thrilled to announce that it has signed a partnership with JSP Foundation for its development programs. FIH will be working closely with JSP Foundation for some of its key initiatives for hockey development over the coming months.

- The National Accreditation Board for Hospitals & Healthcare Providers (NABH) and Healthcare Sector Skill Council (HSSC) signed a memorandum of understanding (MoU). The pact between NABH and HSSC aims at recognition of the HSSC certificate for NABH accreditation and develops training programs for skilling, reskilling, and upskilling required for healthcare professionals.

- Oppo India and the Government's Common Service Centre (CSC) Academy have announced training 10,000 women in cybersecurity and cyber wellness in the country. The initiative of the partnership between Oppo India and CSC is to empower rural and semi-urban women through the 'Cyber Sangini' Programme, which is supported by the Ministry of Electronics and IT. It aims to equip the women with the skills and knowledge needed to become certified 'Cyber Sanginis'.

- India and Egypt signed an MOU to facilitate content exchange, capacity building, and Co-Productions between Prasar Bharati and the National Media Authority of Egypt. The MoU was signed by Union Minister of Information & Broadcasting, Youth Affairs, and Sports Anurag Singh Thakur, and Minister of Foreign Affairs, Government of Egypt, Sameh Hassan Shoukry. The MoUs were exchanged between the two countries in the presence of the Prime Minister of India and the President of Egypt following the delegation-level talks between the two sides at Hyderabad House in New Delhi.

- Atal Innovation Mission NITI Aayog, Central Board of Secondary Education - Ministry of Education, and Intel India have collaborated to bring a change in the education sector by embedding future skills such as AI and Tinkering in the formal curriculum. The larger aim is to align the NEP 2020's guidance to increase the pace of tech integration for youth, the need to bridge the future skills gap in the country, and optimize the current infrastructure (ATLs, etc.) towards making India AIready. Together, they launched the AIoT Integration in School Curriculum in September 2022 and initiated a pilot.

- Defence PSU Garden Reach Shipbuilders and Engineers (GRSE) Ltd has signed a memorandum of understanding (MoU) with Rolls Royce Solutions of Germany for manufacture of high-quality marine diesel engines at the former's plant in Ranchi, an official said. "The MoU deals with transfer of technology related to engine assembly, painting, parts sourcing and after-sales service for these engines that are to be assembled at GRSE's Diesel Engine Plant in Ranchi," the company official said in a statement. The Indian Navy's Chief of Material Vice Admiral Sandeep Naithani was present at the signing of the MoU.

- Bank of Singapore (BoS), the private banking arm of Oversea-Chinese Banking Corporation (OCBC), announced that it has appointed Jason Moo as its new CEO. BoS's announcement comes after Bloomberg's article on Dec 26, 2022. Moo will succeed Bahren Shaari officially from March 6 onwards.

- Indian Space Research Organization (ISRO) and Microsoft signed a Memorandum of Understanding (MoU) to help Indian Space tech start-ups with technology tools, go-to-market support, and mentoring to help them scale and become business ready. Through this MoU, the space tech startups identified by ISRO will be onboarded onto the Microsoft for Startups Founders Hub.

- Nutrition company Herbalife Nutrition India Private Limited is partnering with international women's cricketer, Smriti Mandhana as a 'nutrition sponsor'. She has had an incredible journey, taking the cricket world by storm with her batting performances. Currently, she is the vice-captain of the Indian women's national cricket team.

Ranks and Reports

- According to Paris-based Reporters Without Borders (RSF), a total of 1,668 Journalists have been killed worldwide with murders, contract killings, ambushes, war zone deaths, and fatal injuries. These journalists have been killed in connection with their work in the last two decades from 2003 to 2022. The reports gave an average of more than 80 journalists being killed every year. Christopher Deloire, RSF Secretary General said that behind the figures, there are the faces, personalities, talent, and commitment of those who have paid with their lives for their information gathering their search for the truth, and their passion for journalism.

- According to a survey by Avtar, a company that specializes in workplace inclusion, Chennai is India's top city for women's employment. Pune, Bengaluru, Hyderabad, and Mumbai are the next best cities for women's employment.

- Power Grid Corporation of India Limited (POWERGRID) has been ranked 1st in Services Sectors across categories Gross Block, Value Addition, Net Profit, Net Worth, Dividend Declaration, and Contribution to the Central Exchequer and has also been ranked 3rd among the Top 10 profit-making Closes.

- Delhi was the most polluted city in India in 2022 with PM 2.5 levels more than double the safe limit and the third highest average PM10 concentration. Among the most polluted cities with respect to PM2.5 levels, Delhi (99.71 micrograms per cubic metre) ranked first, Haryana's Faridabad (95.64 micrograms per cubic metre) ranked second and Uttar Pradesh's Ghaziabad (91.25 micrograms per cubic metre) third.

- The richest one per cent of Indians own over 13 times more wealth than the bottom 50 per cent, according to a report by Oxfam India. The top five per cent own 61.7 per cent of the total wealth, nearly 20 times more than the 3 per cent owned by the bottom half. According to the "Survival of the Richest: The India Supplement", released by the non-government organization (NGO), wealth inequality gets denser on the top. More than half of the wealth of the top 10 per cent of richest Indians is owned by the top 1 per cent. The combined wealth of India's 100 richest persons reached Rs 54.12 lakh crore in 2022. The total wealth of the 10 richest Indian stood at Rs 27.52 lakh crore in 2022, a 32.8% rise from 2021.

- The world faces a set of risks that feel both wholly new and eerily familiar. The Global Risks Report 2023 explores some of the most severe risks we may face over the next decade. As we stand on the edge of a low growth and low-cooperation era, tougher trade-offs risk eroding climate action, human development and future resilience. The World Economic Forum taking place in Davos, Switzerland released the 18th edition of the Global Risk Report 2023 based on the 2022-2023 Global Risks Perception Survey (GRPS).

- Bollywood actor Shah Rukh Khan with his more than three decades of work in the film industry has garnered millions of fans all over the world and an estimated net worth of ₹627 million ($770 million), making him the richest actor in Asia and fourth richest actor all over the world. Beating fellow immensely famous and cult actors like Tom Cruise, Jackie Chan, and George Clooney, Shah Rukh Khan took the fourth position in the list of eight richest actors of the world released by World of Statistics.

- The Global Firepower Index ranks the countries based on their potential military strength. India is ranked fourth in the index. The Global Firepower Index ranked 145 countries. The countries were evaluated based on prolonged offensive and defensive military campaigns. The Global Firepower Index, 2022, puts the US at the top, Russia at the second spot, China at No. 3, and India at No. 4. Tata Consultancy Services and Infosys grew their brand value to retain their positions as the second and third most valuable IT services brands, according to the 'IT Services 25' list prepared by UK-based consultancy Brand Finance for the year 2023. Accenture retained the top slot for the fifth year straight, with a brand valued at $39.8 billion. It is the strongest IT services brand in the ranking with a Brand Strength Index (BSI) score of 87.8 out of 100 and a corresponding AAA brand rating.

- Ernst & Young, released a report titled India@100: Realizing the potential of a US $26 trillion economies. According to the estimates Indian economy will reach GDP size of US $26 trillion by 2047, the 100th year of the country's independence. The per capita income is expected to increase to US$15,000, putting the country among the ranks of developed economies.

- Reliance Jio has been ranked as the strongest brand in India and placed ninth among the world's strongest brands, according to the latest report 'Global 500 2023' published by Brand Finance. 'Jio' was placed ninth among the world's strongest brands ahead of brands like EY, Coca Cola, Accenture and Porsche, and behind the likes of Google, YouTube, Deloitte and Instagram. With a Brand Strength Index of 90.2, Jio is the only brand of India among the world's strongest 25 brands, according to the Brand Finance listing.

- India has emerged as one of the top three countries in the world where the area under organic agriculture expanded the maximum in 2020. The total increase under organic cultivation globally in 2020 was 3 million hectares (mh), out of which Argentina accounted for 7,81,000 hectares (up by 21 per cent), followed by Uruguay at 5,89,000 hectares (28 per cent) and India at 3,59,000 hectares.

- After his meteoric rise to the position of the world's third wealthiest man, Gautam Adani has been dragged down to the seventh position on Forbes' rich list by Hindenburg's damning report. The serious claims have triggered off a storm as Indian index Sensex opened 1,000 points lower, and market regulator SEBI increased scrutiny against the Adani Group.

- Gautam Adani has fallen out of the exclusive group of the top 10 wealthiest billionaires in the world after losing $36 billion of his wealth so far in January as a result of a collapse in firm share prices in the wake of the Hindenburg report. According to Bloomberg Billionaires Index, the Indian tycoon, 60, who has his headquarters in Ahmedabad, is currently ranked 11th in terms of wealth with $84.4 billion in assets.

Sports Current Affairs

- Hockey Haryana's women's team won the Khelo India Youth Games 2022 Women's Under 18 Qualifiers after defeating Madhya Pradesh (2-0) in the final at Bhubaneswar. In the final match, Pooja and Gurmail Kaur scored a goal each for Haryana to end the contest in their favour.

- In Hockey, Madhya Pradesh defeated Odisha 6-5 to clinch Khelo India Youth Games 2022 Men's Under-18 Qualifiers title in Bhubaneswar. In a thrilling final, Jamir Mohammad was the star of the final, scoring a hat-trick, while Ali Ahmed, Mohammad Zaid Khan and captain Ankit Pal scored one goal each for Madhya Pradesh.

- Former World rapid champion K. Humpy produced a superlative performance to claim India's first-ever silver medal from the World blitz chess championship that concluded in Almaty, Kazakhstan. Humpy defeated China's Zhongyi Tan to win Silver in the 17th and final round.

- Nineteen-year-old Kolkata-based chess player, Koustav Chatterjee became India's 78th Grandmaster. He is also the tenth GM from West Bengal. Koustav earned his first GM norm in October 2021 at a Grandmasters' chess tournament in Bangladesh.

- The Board of Control for Cricket in India (BCCI) announced that Yo-Yo Test and Dexa will be a part of the selection criteria. BCCI has also discussed the player's availability, workload management, and fitness parameters in the team review meeting along with the roadmap of the ICC Cricket World Cup 2023. ICC Cricket World Cup is scheduled in October and November, and it is to be hosted by India.

- Saurashtra's Jaydev Unadkat made a slice of Ranji Trophy history, becoming the first bowler to take a hattrick in the opening over. The left-arm pacer destroyed Delhi by adding two more in the next over in a careerbest eight-wicket haul in the Elite Group B match in Rajkot. Unadkat's hat-trick victims included opener Dhruv Shorey, Vaibhav Rawal and young Delhi captain Yash Dhull, all of whom departed for duck.

- Odisha Chief Minister Naveen Patnaik on Thursday inaugurated one of the largest hockey stadiums in India in Rourkela ahead of the Men's Hockey World Cup 2023. Built at an estimated cost of ₹261 crore, the stadium, located in Sundargarh district, has been christened as Birsa Munda Hockey Stadium Complex. It has been built in 50 acres in a record 15 months-time with a seating capacity of 20,000. The stadium also has practice centres adjacent to it with certified turfs and lighting. The State has also built a World Cup village, which has 225 rooms to house the players and officials, within nine months.

- Australia's Belinda Clark has become the first female cricketer to have a statue cast in her honour, a bronze sculpture of the trailblazing former captain unveiled outside Sydney Cricket Ground. Clark played 15 tests and over 100 limited overs matches between 1991-2005, and became the first cricketer to score a double hundred in one-day internationals when she made an unbeaten 229 against Denmark in 1997.

- Prinesh M became India's 79th Grandmaster, having completed his three norms prior to this event. IM Prinesh M emerged as the winner of the Rilton Cup, the first tournament of the FIDE Circuit. The 16-year-old from India, seeded 22nd, made a clean sweep of the field in Stockholm, winning eight games and finishing a full point ahead of IM Kan Kochukaru (Sweden) and GM Nikita Mesko's (Latvia).

- Indian Tennis Player Sania Mirza (36-year-old), the former doubles World No. 1, has confirmed her retirement from professional Tennis. She announced that the Dubai Tennis Championships, a Women's Tennis Association (WTA) 1000 event in Dubai in February 2023 will be her last match. Prior to her last appearance, she is going to play in women's doubles at the Australian Open in 16 to 29 January 2023 alongside Kazakhstan's Anna Danilina.

- Novak Djokovic has defeated America's Sebastian Karda in a nerve-wracking final to win the Adelaide International men's singles title. Djokovic also equaled Rafael Nadal's tally of 92 ATP singles titles in the Open Era. Nadal and Djokovic are joint-fourth in the list after Jimmy Connors (109), Roger Federer (103) and Ivan Lendl (94). In the women's final at Adelaide International 1, Aryna Sabalenka won the women's singles by defeating Linda Noskova of the Czech Republic. This was her 11th WTA Tour singles title.

- Cricket South Africa (CSA) has confirmed that Proteas all-rounder Dwaine Pretorius has retired from international cricket with immediate effect. Since making his international debut in 2016, the 33-year-old has represented South Africa across all three formats in 30 T20 Internationals (T20I), 27 One-Day Internationals (ODI) and three Tests.

- Anahat Singh won the Girl's U-15 squash title at British Junior Open Tournament. Anahat Singh was also one of the youngest players at the Commonwealth Games 2022. She won one of the most prestigious tournaments of the season in Birmingham, U.K.

- India VS Sri Lanka: Indian Cricketer, Virat Kohli has recorded the first century by an Indian in 2023 against Sri Lanka in the first One-Day International at the Baraspara Cricket Stadium in Guwahati. He made 113 off 87 balls. Kohli's 45th ODI ton helped him equal Sachin Tendulkar's record for most centuries at home in ODI cricket. While Tendulkar had 20 centuries in 160 innings at home, Kohli smashed his 20 ton in his 99th innings at home.

- Surya Kumar Yadav has become the fastest player to reach 1,500 runs in T20 International cricket in terms of balls faced. The took only 843 balls to reach this landmark. In 45 matches and 43 innings, Suryakumar has scored 1,578 runs at an average of 46.41. He has three centuries and 13 half-centuries in the format, with the best individual score of 117.

- The Khelo India Senior Women National Kho Kho league is to take place at Chandigarh University, Punjab. It will be held from 10th to 13th January 2023 in three phases. It is being organized by the Kho-Kho Federation of India with prize money of Rs 18 Lakh.

- Harry Brook received the ICC Men's Player of the Month award after a blistering run of scores that helped England claim a historic World Test Championship (WTC) series victory in Pakistan. On the other hand, Australia's Ashleigh Gardner bagged the ICC Women's Player of the Month award for her contributions with bat and ball in the T20I series against India.
- Falak Mumtaz, an 11-year-old girl from Jammu and Kashmir has bagged a gold medal in National Sqay Championship. Falak Mumtaz has achieved a gold medal in the National Sqay Championship which was held in Jammu. She is currently studying sixth standard at Aisha Ali Academy in Kulgam.
- In Cricket, India scripted history by defeating Sri Lanka by the largest ever margin of 317 runs in the third and final ODI in Thiruvananthpuram, Kerala. With this, India also clean sweeped the series by 3-0. Previous record of a win by a largest ever margin was with the New Zealand, for 290-run win over Ireland in 2008.
- Star cricketer Virat Kohli became the fifth-highest runscorer in history of ODI cricket, overtaking Sri Lankan legend Mahela Jayawardene to enter into top-five. At the time of becoming the fifth-highest run-scorer, Virat had 12,652 runs in 268 ODIs at an average of 57.78, with 45 tons and 65 half-century. His best score in the format is 183.
- The Board of Control for Cricket in India (BCCI) has announced that Viacom 18 have grabbed the media rights for the upcoming Women's IPL for a whopping Rs 951 crore for five years, pipping other bidders, including Disney Star and Sony, in the auction. The auction for the T20 League was conducted by the cricket board in Mumbai.
- Barcelona have won the Spanish Super Cup for the first time since the competition was revamped and moved to Saudi Arabia with a 3-1 victory over Real Madrid. Robert Lewandowski, Gavi and Pedri scored a goal each at King Fahd Stadium in Riyadh to give Barcelona its first Super Cup trophy since 2018, and the first since the tournament's Final-Four format began in 2020 in a lucrative deal for the Spanish football federation.

- Indian batter Shubman Gill has smashed three sixes on the trot to reach his double hundred (208 off 149 with 4s-19 and 6s-9) and become only the eighth and the youngest player (23 years) in ODI history. He also became the fastest Indian to complete 1000 runs in ODIs as he reached the mark in 19 innings, surpassing the likes of Virat Kohli and Shikhar Dhawan.

- Hashim Amla ended his 22-year playing career, with his legacy secure as one of South Africa's all-time cricketing greats. Amla was a key member of one of South Africa's most powerful teams when they clinched the Test championship mace with a series win in England in 2012.

- The Rwanda fast bowler, Geovanis Uwase has been suspended by ICC from bowling in international cricket with immediate effect after her action was found illegal at Under-19 Women's T20 World Cup. The decision was taken by the Event Panel, which comprises members of the ICC Panel of Human Movement Specialists.

- Indian captain Rohit Sharma has shattered a longstanding record held by MS Dhoni to become India's most prolific six-hitter in the history of ODI cricket. At the Rajiv Gandhi Stadium in Hyderabad, Rohit achieved this remarkable feat during the first ODI between India and New Zealand. The Indian captain's knock included two maximums, breaking MS Dhoni's long-standing record. Rohit is now India's leading six-getter in the history of ODI cricket, with a total of 125 sixes to his name.

- The global governing body of cricket, the International Cricket Council (ICC), reportedly lost nearly $2.5 million in online scam last year. The incident of phishing, which originated in the US, took place last year. As per reports, the ICC was repeatedly cheated by the scamster not once, not twice, but four times. Surprisingly, the authorities at the ICC's Dubai office did not have a clue that they were being cheated.

- Shuttler Kunlavut Vitidsarn from Thailand won the India Open Badminton Championship 2023 by defeating Denmark's Viktor Axelsen in the men's singles by 22-20, 10-21 and 21-12. In the Women's Singles category, An Seyoung of South Korea won the title by defeating Japanese Akane Yamaguchi by 15-21 21-16, and 21-12.

- The International Cricket Council's (ICC) 92.2 million followers across Instagram, Facebook, Twitter, TikTok and YouTube makes it the most followed international sports federation on social media, according to a study from BCW Sports. The ICC increased its following by 16 per cent, putting it a massive 40.8 million followers ahead of second-placed Fifa (51.4 million).
- Germany beat Belgium 5-4 in the penalty shootout to win the FIH Men's Hockey World Cup 2023 at the Kalinga Stadium in Bhubaneswar, India. The scores were level at the end of regulation time at 3-3. This is Germany's third Hockey World Cup title after they won it in 2002 and 2006.
- India beat England in the first-ever ICC U-19 Women's T20 World Cup final in Potchefstroom, South Africa. India bowled out England for a paltry 68 and won by 7 wkts. This is the first ICC trophy India has won in women's cricket. The Indian women's cricket team has never won a World Cup at any level. England captain and stellar all-rounder Grace Scrivens has been named Player of the Tournament after a run of outstanding performances with bat and ball. Titas Sadhu of India poses after being named Player of the Match following the ICC Women's U19 T20 World Cup 2023 Final match.
- Veteran Indian opener Murali Vijay has announced his retirement from all forms of international cricket. He last played for India in December 2018 during the BorderGavaskar Test series against Australia. Murali appeared in 61 Tests, 17 ODIs and nine T20Is for India during his international career that began back in 2008 when he came in for Gautam Gambhir in the playing XI of the final Test match of Border-Gavaskar Test series against Australia in Nagpur.

Summits And Conferences

- Indian Science Congress's 108th edition was officially inaugrated by Prime Minister Narendra Modi. Rashtrasant Tukadoji Maharaj Nagpur University is hosting the five-day 108th session of ISC as it commemorates its centennial.He emphasised the nation's expanding energy requirements and urged the scientific community to develop any advances in the area that would help the nation.
- Ministry of Jal Shakti organized the "1st All India Annual State Minister Conference on Water" with the theme of "Water Vision@2027" in Bhopal, Madhya Pradesh on 5th and 6th January 2023. Chief Minister of Madhya Pradesh, Shivaraj

Singh Chouhan, and Union Minister of Jal Shakti Gajendra Singh Shekhawat felicitated the occasion.

- India will host 'The Voice of Global South' Summit on January 12-13, Foreign Secretary Vinay Kwatra said. As many as 120 countries will participate in the summit. The virtual summit is significant as India currently holds the presidency of the G20 group and Prime Minister Narendra Modi had earlier indicated that priorities would be shaped in consultation with developing countries. The 'Voice of Global South Summit' under the theme 'Unity of Voice, Unity of Purpose' envisages bringing together countries of the Global South to share their perspectives and priorities on a common platform.

- Dr. Jitendra Singh, the Union Minister for Science and Technology, launched the Geospatial Hackathon to encourage innovation and start-ups in India's geospatial ecosystem. Speaking at the event in New Delhi, Dr. Singh stated that the hackathon's goal was to encourage collaborations between the public and private geospatial sectors as well as to develop the nation's environment for geospatial start-ups.

- The first 15 meetings of the Business 20 (B20) India Inception Meeting will be held in Gandhinagar from January 22nd to 24th, 2023. The Gujarat Government to host a dinner for G20 delegates followed by a delegation visiting the Dandi Kutir. India has been assumed as the G20 under the leadership of Prime Minister Narendra Modi. The nation aspires to play an important role on the world stage by finding practical global solutions for the welfare of all. The G20 chairman for India is a historic event as it comes while celebrating the 'Azadi Ka Amrit Mahotsav'.

- A two-day Think-20 summit under the auspices of the G20 will bring together prominent individuals from around the world to debate a range of issues, including "Global Governance with LiFE, Values, and Wellbeing."

- The sole centre in India with a focus on healthcare and life sciences will be created in Hyderabad as the World Economic Forum Centre for the Fourth Industrial Revolution (C4IR Telangana).

- The Election Commission of India (ECI) is hosting the 2nd International Conference on the theme 'Use of Technology and Elections Integrity' in New Delhi from

23rd to 24th January 2023. ECI is leading the Cohort on Elections Integrity which was established as a follow-up to the 'Summit for Democracy' held virtually in December 2021.

- In the 12th Session of the Intergovernmental Technical Working Group (ITWG) on Animal Genetic Resources (AnGR) India was elected as Vice-Chair and represented Asia & Pacific region. Dr. B N Tripathi, Deputy Director General (Animal Sciences), ICAR, and the National Coordinator, vice-chaired the Session and also act as Rapporteur. The 12th Session of the Intergovernmental Technical Working Group (ITWG) on Animal Genetic Resources was held in Rome from 18th January to 20th January 2023.

- The inaugural India Stack Developer Conference was held on January 25 in New Delhi. The conference focused on strategies for ensuring greater global adoption of Indian digital products. More than 100 digital leaders from business, government, academia, startups, and unicorns attended the conference. The Conference had also extended invitations to representatives from G20 nations and the G20 Secretariat.

- India's G-20 Sherpa Amitabh Kant inaugurated India's first Model G-20 Summit organized by Rambhau Mhalgi Prabodhini's Indian Institute of Democratic Leadership. The two-day Model G-20 Summit has been organized at the Rambhau Mhalgi Prabodhini's Uttan campus in Mumbai to celebrate India's presidency and take the idea of G-20 to the youth.

Awards & Recognition

- Odisha won the UN-Habitat's World Habitat Awards 2023 for Jaga Mission, a 5 T initiative of the state. The awards recognise and highlight innovative, outstanding and revolutionary housing ideas, projects and programmed from across the world. The Jaga mission is the land titling and slum upgrading program that aims at empowering the lives of slum dwellers.

- Writer Ambikasuthan Mangad has been selected for Odakuzhal Award 2022 for his collection of short stories titled Pranavayu. The award consists of Rs 30,000, citation, and plaque. Instituted by the Guruvayurappan Trust, the award is being given for the best collection of short stories in Malayalam. The award will be presented on the occasion of the 45th death anniversary of Mahakavi G. Sankara Kurup, who established the Guruvayurappan Trust, on February 2 at the Ernakulam Samastha Kerala Sahithya Parishad building here. Literary critic Dr. M. Leelavathi will present the award to Ambikasuthan Mangad.

- The recipients of the state's top civil honours for 2022-2023 were revealed by the Assam government. The Assam government presented awards in the Asom Baibhav, Asom Sourav, and Asom Gourav categories. The chief minister of Assam, Himanta Biswa Sarma, revealed the beneficiaries of the civil awards that will be given out by the state.

- The Harvard Law School Center on the Legal Profession (HLS CLP) has announced Chief Justice of India Dr. DY Chandrachud as the 2022 recipient of its "Award for Global Leadership" in recognition of his lifetime service to the legal profession in India and across the world. The award will be presented to him in a virtual event on 11th January 2023.

- University of Kerala bagged the 'Overall Championship' at Padma Tarang, the 36th Inter University South Zone Youth Festival at Sri Padmavati Mahila Viswa Vidyalayam (SPMVV) in Tirupati. Mahatma Gandhi University, Kottayam, came the runners-up. With more than 700 registered participants from universities across South India converging on the campus.

- e-NAM, a flagship initiative of the Ministry of Agriculture and Farmers Welfare, has won the Platinum Award in the Digital Empowerment of Citizens Category in Digital India Awards 2022 held in New Delhi. The President of India, Smt. Droupadi Murmu, as Chief Guest of the event, has conferred the Digital India Awards, 2022.

- Vivek Agnihotri's film 'The Kashmir Files' has been shortlisted for Oscars 2023. That means now this film has qualified to get an Oscar. Actors Anupam Kher, Mithun Chakraborthy, Darshan Kumar and Pallavi Joshi are also shortlisted for the best actor category. After RRR, there are three major entries from the Hindi film industry on the list namely The Kashmir Films, Gangubai Kathiawadi, and Rocketry.

- Actress Aparna Sen was honored with the lifetime achievement award at the opening ceremony of the 15th Edition of the Jaipur International Film Festival. At the event, 282 films from 63 countries will be screened. Aparna Sen debuted in Satyajit Ray's Teen Kanya in 1961. The Government of India honored Aparna Sen with Padma Shri in 1987.

- Over 1,000 Indian peacekeepers serving with the United Nations Mission in South Sudan (UNMISS) have been honoured with the prestigious UN medals at an award ceremony where the parade was led for the first time by a woman officer of the Indian Army.

- Noted writer K Venu was conferred with Federal Bank Literary Award 2022 for his autobiography 'Oranweshananthinte Katha.' Venu received the award from Balagopal Chandrasekhar, Chairman and Independent Director of Federal Bank, at a special event held as part of the Kerala Literature Festival.

- Rajasthani film, Naanera, directed by Deepankar Prakash bagged the 'Golden Kailasha' award for the best movie at the Ajanta-Ellora Film Festival. Naanera (Grandfather's House) revolves around Manish (Main Character). After the death of his father, Manish's uncle starts taking his life's decisions.

- The New Goa Manohar International Airport (MIA), built by the GMR Goa International Airport Ltd (GGIAL), a subsidiary of GMR Airports Infrastructure Limited, won the prestigious "Best Sustainable Greenfield Airport" award under Aviation Sustainability and Environment at ASSOCHAM 14th International Conference-cum-Awards for Civil Aviation 2023 at New Delhi.

- Himalayan Cataract Project Co-Founder Dr Sanduk Ruit has won the ISA Award for Service to Humanity, a top civilian award of Bahrain. The award carries a cash prize of USD 1 million, a certificate of merit and a gold medal. He is pioneer in delivering high-quality microsurgical procedures in remote eye camps. He made modern eye care affordable and accessible to countries in Asia, Africa and Latin America.

- ESAF Small Finance Bank has bagged the prestigious Inclusive Finance India Awards 2022 for its contributions in advancing the goal of financial inclusion and supporting inclusive growth. This award is a recognition of ESAF's unique spectrum of Financial Inclusion projects ESAF Dhansree, ESAF Udyog Jyothi, LSEDP (Local Sustainable Economic Development Project), ESAF Balajyothi, ESAF Vayojyothi, and ESAF Garshom.

- R Vishnu Prassad was awarded "The most distinguished scientist of the year 2022" at Vigyan bhawan, Delhi. Prassad, a scientist with 69 patents has been honored with the Indian Achievers Award as the most distinguished scientist of the year.

- Two Indian films bagged awards for the best script writer and best actress in the Asian Film Competition section at the 21st Dhaka International Film Festival (DIFF), Bangladesh concluded. Anik Dutta directed film Aparajito (The Undefeated) got the best scriptwriting award while Ketaki Narayan was judged the best actress for her role in Krishnendu Kalesh directed film Prappeda (Hawk's Muffin).

- The Song 'Naatu Naatu' from India's blockbuster film RRR and two documentaries from the country 'All That Breathes' and 'The Elephant Whisperers' have made it to the final nominations list at the 95th edition of the Academy Awards. However, India's official entry Chhello Show (Last Film Show), Gujarati language coming-of-age drama did not score a nomination in the Best International Feature category at the 95th Academy Awards.

- Hindustani vocalist Padma Vibhushan, Dr. Prabha Atre was conferred with the the Pandit Hariprasad Chaurasia Lifetime Achievement Award at the hands of Maharashtra Chief Minister Eknath Shinde.

- New Zealand Cricket (NZC) has announced that outstanding women's cricketer will be honoured with the inaugural Debbie Hockley Medal at this year's annual cricket awards ceremony. Debbie, regarded as one of the world's best batters during her playing days and one of the finest to have played the game, played 118 ODIs and 19 Tests for New Zealand from 1979 to 2000.

- The President of India Droupadi Murmu has awarded the RPF/RPSF personnel with Jeevan Raksha Padak awards to Jaipal Singh, Head Constable/ Northern Railway, Surendra Kumar, Constable/Northern Railway, and Bhuda Ram Saini, Constable/7th BN/RPSF.

Important Days

- The Government of India sponsored the proposal for International Year of Millets (IYM) 2023 which was accepted by the United Nations General Assembly (UNGA). The declaration has been instrumental for the Government of India to be at the forefront in celebrating the IYM. PM Narendra Modi has also shared his vision to make IYM 2023 a 'People's Movement' alongside positioning India as the 'Global Hub for Millets'.

- Global Family Day is celebrated on January 1, each year. The day creates a sense of unity, community and brotherhood across nations and cultures through the idea of families. This day is celebrated to discourage unwarranted negative attitudes towards other cultures, nations, which may breed hatred, encourage social aloofness and lead to violence.

- World Braille Day, marked on January 4, emphasises the significance of Braille as a form of communication for the partially sighted and blind. The United Nations has been commemorating the day since 2019. World Braille Day also commemorates the birth anniversary of Louis Braille, who was born on January 4, 1809. After losing his sight during childhood, the French educator devised the Braille technique.

- The World Day of War Orphans is observed on January 6 every year with an aim to raise awareness about children orphaned in wars. These children are subjected to hardships that are more than just physical neglect after losing their caregivers. It is an important event to note that the aftermaths of war are not just harsh on a single part of society.

- The Department for Promotion of Industry and Internal Trade (DPIIT), Ministry of Commerce and Industry is organizing Startup India Innovation Week from 10th January 2023 to 16th January 2023 to celebrate the Indian Startup Ecosystem as well as National Startup Day (16th January 2023). The National Human Trafficking Awareness Day is observed every year in the United States on 11th January. The day is dedicated to raising awareness about human trafficking. Even though the entire month of January has been recognized as the National Slavery and Human Trafficking Prevention Month, January 11 specifically aims towards the prevention of illegal practices.

- Ministry of Road Transport & Highways, Government of India is observing the Road Safety Week from 11th to 17th January 2023, under "Swachhata Pakhwada", to propagate the cause of safer roads for all.

- The Armed Forces Veterans Day is celebrated on 14th January since 1953, the First Indian Commander in Chief (C-in-C) of Indian Army- Field Marshal KM

Cariappa, who led Indian Forces to Victory in the 1947 war, had formally retired from the Services. The Day is celebrated as Armed Forces Veterans Day and dedicated to our esteemed Veterans. This year 7th Armed Forces Veterans Day celebrates on 2023.

- Indian army day 2023 is celebrated on 15th January 2023 and it mark the 75th anniversary of the Indian army day. Every year on January 15, India celebrates its Army Day. It is the day on which Field Marshal Kodandera M. Cariappa (then a Lieutenant General) took over as the first CommanderinChief of the Indian Army from the last British CommanderinChief of India, General Fransis Bucher in the year 1949.

- 16th January, the founding day of Startup India is commemmorated as the National Startup Day. The event is being celebrated since 2022. Prime Minister Narendra Modi made the announceent last year by calling startups as backbone of new India. The Central government has planned several events this year to celebrate the National startup day across the country as a part of the Azadi Ka Amrit Mahotsav. To celebrate the spirit of Indian startup ecosystem and mark this momentous day, DPIIT (Department for Promotion of Industry and Internal Trade) is organising Startup India Innovation Week from 10th - 16th January 2023.

- 18th National Disaster Response Force Day is celebrated on January 19, 2023, by the National Disaster Response Force (NDRF). The day has been celebrated on this day since 2006 when the rescue force was officially formed. The specialised, multi-skilled rescue force is made up of battalions from the Border Security Force (BSF), Central Reserve Police Force (CRPF), Central Industrial Security Force (CISF), IndoTibetan Border Police (ITBP), Sashastra Seema Bal (SSB) and the Assam Rifles.

- The United Nations General Assembly has proclaimed 24 January as International Day of Education, in celebration of the role of education for peace and development. The fifth International Day of Education will be celebrated on 24 January 2023 under the theme "to invest in people, prioritize education".

- On January 24, the nation celebrates National Girl Child Day. This day was established in 2008 by the Ministry of Women and Child Development. The Ministry of Education will host a celebration with the theme "Self Defence Training for Girls."

- Election Commission of India is celebrating 13th National Voters' Day on 25th January 2023. This day is celebrated on 25 January to mark the foundation day of the Election Commission of India. The theme for this year's NVD, 'Nothing Like Voting, I Vote for Sure' is dedicated to voters which conveys individual's feeling and aspiration towards participation in the electoral process through power of their vote. Since 2011, National Voters' Day has been celebrated on January 25 every year, all across the country to mark the foundation day of the Election Commission of India, i.e. 25th January 1950.

- India Energy Week 2023 is going to be hosted in Bengaluru from 6th to 8th February 2023. The Union Minister of Petroleum and Natural Gas, Housing and Urban Affairs, Government of India Hardeep S. Puri inaugurated the demo run of an Inland Water Vessel powered by Methanol blended Diesel (MD15).

- The World Customs Organisation (WCO) marks International Customs Day on 26th January every year. The occasion commemorates the WCO's maiden session held in 1953. This year, the theme of International Customs Day is 'Nurturing the next generation: Promoting a culture of knowledgesharing and professional pride in Customs.'

- Every year, International Holocaust Remembrance Day is observed on January 27 to reflect on the atrocities inflicted by Adolf Hitler, which resulted in the deaths of an estimated six million Jews. The day commemorates the liberation of Auschwitz-Birkenau in January 1945 from Nazi control. The theme "Home and Belonging" guides United Nations Holocaust remembrance and education in 2023.

- Data Protection Day, or Data Privacy Day, is celebrated on January 28. The aim is to create more awareness about the right to data protection and the various ways in which people can keep their data more safe. Let's first understand the history and significance. The theme for this year is 'Think Privacy First'. In this digital age, it is pragmatic to prioritize data privacy, both for individuals and businesses.

- On January 30, 2023, India observed Martyrs' Day or Shaheed Diwas to pay tribute to all the freedom fighters who sacrificed their lives for the country. The day is also marked as the death anniversary of the nation's 'Bapu', Mahatma Gandhi. On this day in 1948, Gandhi was assassinated by Nathuram Godse in the compound of Birla House after one of his routine multi-faith prayer meetings.

- World Leprosy Day (WLD) is celebrated on the last Sunday of January. In 2023, World Leprosy Day is observed on 29 January. This international day is an opportunity to celebrate people who have experienced leprosy, raise awareness of the disease, and call for an end to leprosy-related stigma and discrimination. This date was chosen by French humanitarian, Raoul Follereau as a tribute to the life of Mahatma Gandhi, who did much work with persons affected by leprosy and died at the end of January in 1948. The theme of World Leprosy Day 2023 is "Act Now. End Leprosy."

- World Neglected Tropical Diseases Day (World NTD Day) is observed on January 30 every year to raise awareness about neglected tropical diseases (NTDs) as a critical public health challenge so that we can progress towards their elimination. 2023 theme is "Act Now. Act Together. Invest in Neglected Tropical Diseases". The proposal to recognise the day was floated by the United Arab Emirates. It was adopted unanimously by the delegates. The first World NTD Day was celebrated informally in 2020.

Defence Current Affairs

- Defence Research and Development Organisation (DRDO) Headquarters in New Delhi has marked the 65th Foundation Day of the Organisation, which is celebrated on 1st January every year. DRDO Chairman Dr S V Kamat addressed the DRDO fraternity on the occasion. He reaffirmed DRDO's commitment towards R&D excellence and briefed about the development of cutting edge technologies for self-reliance in defence.

- Captain Shiva Chauhan from the Corps of Engineers has been posted at a frontline post in Siachen Glacier, in first such operational deployment of an woman Army officer at the world's highest battlefield. The officer was posted at the Kumar post, located at an altitude of around 15,600 feet in Siachen, for a three-month stint after she underwent rigorous training. The training included endurance training, ice wall climbing, avalanche and crevasse rescue and survival drills.

- K9-Vajra: The Defence Ministry has started the process for the procurement of 100 more K9-Vajra tracked self-propelled howitzers which are built in India by Larsen & Toubro (L&T) using technology transferred from South Korean defence major Hanwha Defence.

- India will deploy a platoon of women peacekeepers to UN Mission in Sudan. This will be India's largest single unit of women Peacekeepers in a UN Mission since it deployed the first-ever all-women contingent in Liberia in 2007. The Indian contingent, comprising two officers and 25 Other Ranks, will form part of an Engagement platoon and specialize in Community outreach, though they will be performing extensive security-related tasks as well. The deployment in Abyei will also herald India's intent of increasing significantly the number of Indian women in Peacekeeping contingents.

- Bharat Petroleum Corporation Limited (BPCL), a Maharatna and a Fortune Global 500 Company, has announced the launch of Low Smoke Superior Kerosene Oil (SKO) for the Indian Army in Jammu.

- The Defence Research and Development Organization (DRDO) has developed an unmanned aerial vehicle (UAV) to carry out logistic operations in the Himalayan frontier. The DRDO-developed UAV is capable of flying in the Himalayan Environment with 5 kg of payload and even dropping bombs in the areas required.

- iDEX has signed its 50th SPRINT contract with Sagar Defence for Autonomous Weaponised Boat Swarms for the Indian Navy. Autonomous Weaponised Boat is one of the technologies introduced out of the 75 challenges by the Indian Navy under the Azadi Ka Amrit Mahotsav in 2022. Sagar Defence has developed the country's first Autonomous Weaponised unmanned boat with the capability for swarming. The contract was signed under an Indian Navy project of the Defence India Start-up Challenge (DISC 7) SPRINT initiative.

- Su-30MKI pilot Squadron Leader Chaturvedi will be assigned to the Veer Guardian 2023 in Japan. First female fighter pilot in the Indian Air Force (IAF), squadron commander Avani Chaturvedi, will participate in the inaugural air exercise Veer Guardian 2023. The goal of the exercise is to improve air defence cooperation between Japan and India.

- India successfully carried out a test launch of the tactical ballistic missile Prithvi-II from the Integrated Test Range, Chandipur, Odisha coast. Prithvi-II is an indigenously developed surface-to-surface Missile shortrange ballistic missile (SRBM) and has a range of around 250 km to 350 km.

- Defence Acquisition Council(DAC) approved three proposals worth 4,276 crore rupees to strengthen the country's deterrence and combat readiness. Defence Ministry said, a meeting of Defence Acquisition Council held under the chairmanship of Defence Minister Rajnath Singh. The DAC has accorded approval for procurement of HELINA Anti-Tank Guided Missiles, launchers and associated support equipment which will be integrated to the Advanced Light Helicopter.

- The Defence Acquisition Council (DAC) cleared the proposal for procurement of VSHORAD (IR Homing) missile system under design and development by the Defence Research and Development Organisation(DRD0). In view of the recent developments along the Northern borders(China) there is a need to focus on effective Air Defence (AD) weapon systems which are man portable and can be deployed quickly in rugged terrain and maritime domain.

- The Japan Air Self Defense Force (JASDF) and the Indian Air Force will participate in the joint air exercise "Veer Guardian-2023" starting on January 12 at Hyakuri Air Base in Japan.

- The 23rd of this month will see the Aadi Shaurya - Parv Parakram Ka Tribal Dance Festival and Military Tattoo at Jawaharlal Nehru Stadium in New Delhi. The two-day celebration, according to the Defence Ministry, would display the strength of the Armed Forces and the cultural beauty of India's tribal cultures.

- Indian Coast Guard (ICG) ship 'Kamla Devi' the Fast Patrol Vessel (FPV) which is designed, built, and delivered by Garden Reach Shipbuilders and Engineers (GRSE) Ltd to Indian Coast Guard was commissioned in Kolkata, West Bengal. Indian Coast Guard ship Kamla Devi is officially the fifth and last vessel of the series of FPVs designed and built by GRSE as per the specifications of the Indian Coast Guard.

- Captain Surbhi Jakhmola of the Indian Army's 117 Engineer Regiment will be the first woman officer to be posted on a foreign assignment at the Border Roads Organisation (BR0). The officer will be sent to Bhutan as part of Project Dantak. The Border Roads Organisation (BRO) is an executive road construction force in India that supports the Indian armed forces.

- According to the Ministry of Defence, the 21st edition of "Varuna" the bilateral naval exercise between India and France commenced on the western seaboard.

This edition of the exercise will witness participation of indigenous guided missile stealth destroyer INS Chennai, guided missile frigate INS Teg, maritime patrol aircraft P-8I and Dornier, integral helicopters and MiG29K fighter aircraft. The French Navy will be represented by the aircraft carrier Charles De Gaulle, frigates FS Forbin and Provence, support vessel FS Marne and maritime patrol aircraft Atlantique.

- The Indian Army has organized the second edition of the Hackathon named "SAINYA RANAKSHETRAM 2.0" from October 2022 to January 2023 under the aegis of HQ Army Training Command (ARTRAC). The "SAINYA RANAKSHETRAM 2.0" aims to seek solutions to operational cyber challenges and jump-start and telescope the development time for innovative solutions in the field of Cyber Security.

- Tata Boeing Aerospace Limited (TBAL) has delivered the first fuselage for six AH-64 Apache attack helicopters ordered by the Indian Army from its state-ofthe-art facility in Hyderabad.

- The first joint exercise between the special forces of the Indian and the Egyptian Army, 'Exercise Cyclone - I' started on 14 January at Jaisalmer, Rajasthan, said the Ministry of Defence. The exercise aims to bolster defence co-operation between the two countries and focus on sharing professional skills and interoperability of special forces in desert terrain while undertaking counter terrorism, reconnaissance, raids and other special operations.

- Indian Navy is set to commission the fifth Kalvari class submarine Vagir on 23 Jan 2023. The Chief of the Naval Staff Adm R Hari Kumar will be the Chief Guest for the ceremony. These submarines are being built in India by the Mazagon Dock Shipbuilders Limited (MDL) Mumbai, under collaboration with M/s Naval Group, France. Four of the Kalvari class of submarines have already been commissioned into the Indian Navy.

- Indian Navy has carried out a six-day-long mega military exercise along with the Indian Army and the Indian Air Force near Kakinada in Andhra Pradesh. The "largest" biennial tri-services amphibious exercise AMPHEX 2023 was conducted from January 17 to 22. The exercise is to review the preparedness of the Indian Navy and the Army during the war, national calamities and coastal security enforcement.

- The Indian Air Force (IAF) is set to conduct Exercise PRALAY in the northeastern sector of India amid the unresolved contention with China about differing perceptions regarding the Line of Actual Control (LAC) between the two nations. The exercise will involve major air bases of the IAF in the northeast in addition to the recently deployed drone squadron.

- The 2023 edition of Indian Navy's major maritime exercise Theatre Level Operational Readiness Exercise (TROPEX) is currently underway in the Indian Ocean Region. This operational level exercise is conducted biennially and witnesses participation not only by all Indian Navy units but also of Indian Army, Indian Air Force and Coast Guard assets.

- The Indian Air Force will run the massive air exercise Pralay to assess its operational readiness. The significant exercise will take place near the Line of Actual Control in India's northeast, involving all significant Air Force units.

- The Border Security Force (BSF) announced that in preparation for Republic Day festivities, its troops had begun "Ops Alert" with the goal of enhancing security along the International Border (IB) with Pakistan in the Kutch region of Gujarat and Barmer in Rajasthan.

- The inaugural edition of the 16-day bilateral air exercise between the Indian Air Force and the Japan Air Self Defense Force has concluded in Japan. The exercise, 'Veer Guardian 2023', involved precise planning and skilful execution by both the air forces. The JASDF participated in the exercise with its F-2 and F-15 aircraft, while the IAF contingent participated with the Su-30 MKI aircraft.

- PM Modi released special ₹ 75 Coins on the Occasion of completion of 75 years of National Cadet Corps (NCC) at the Delhi NCC Event. Defence Minister Rajnath Singh and Chief of Defence Staff (CDS) of India Lt. Gen Anil Chauhan were also present at the Delhi NCC event. The Yuva Shakti of India is what is propelling the nation's progress, according to Prime Minister Narendra Modi, who made the statement at the NCC rally.

- Air Marshal A P Singh has been appointed as the new Vice Chief of the Indian Air Force. He will succeed Air Marshal Sandeep Singh, who will retire from service. Air Marshal A P Singh is currently serving as the Air Officer Commanding-in-Chief of the Central Air Command. He will take charge as the Vice Chief on

1st Feb 2023. He was commissioned into the fighter stream of the IAF on December 21, 1984.

Science and Technology

- Indian Space and Research Organization (ISRO), National Centre for Earth Sciences (NCES), and the Andhra University (AU) have researched and concluded that constant rip current zones at blue flag-certified Rushikonda beach and RK Beach have become a danger to the beach visitors. Between 2012 to 2022, over 200 people drowned in the sea at various beaches in and around Visakhapatnam and 60 percent of deaths occurred in RK Beach.

- In 2022, the Indian Space Research Organization (ISRO) reached new heights as it experimented with new tests to confirm its human spaceflight mission, built new facilities to train its astronauts, and created a new connection with the private sector by putting India's first privately made rocket to the test. The year 2023 won't be any different. Instead, since the roster is set, it might be a year of bigger, bolder, and braver expeditions from India to space.

- Union Minister Dr Jitendra Singh today inaugurated "National Genome Editing & Training Centre" at National Agri-food Biotechnology Institute (NABI) Mohali, Punjab. The Minister also, at the same time, inaugurated a 4-day International Conference on Food and Nutritional Security 2023 iFANS

- The National Council of Science Museums hosted Astro Tourism - A Sky Gazing event at Delhi's India Gate in collaboration with the Nehru Memorial Museum and Library. Arjun Ram Meghwal, minister of state for culture, gave the event's opening remarks.

- Indian Space Research Organization (ISRO) launch vehicle will carry a satellite built by 750 girls attending government schools across the nation, according to Space Kidz India, a Chennai-based space tech business.

- An Indian American aerospace industry expert has been appointed as NASA's new chief technologist to serve as principal advisor to Administrator Bill Nelson on technology policy and programmed at the space agency's headquarters. A.C. Charania joined the space agency in his new role on January 3. He replaces another

Indian American scientist Bhavya Lal, who served as acting chief technologist prior to the former's appointment.

- Central Mine Planning and Design Institute Limited (CMPDIL) has invented a "System and Method for Controlling Generation and Movement of Fugitive Dust" and obtained a patent for the same in December 2022. This system is developed to be used in mines, thermal power plants, railway sidings, ports, and construction sites where coal and other minerals or fugitive materials are stored in the open sky. The system will reduce dust generation from open source as well as provide noise attenuation.
- A 'green' comet from the outer solar system will pass through our area of space for the first time in 50,000 years this month. It is providing skywatchers with a oncein-a-lifetime opportunity to see this celestial phenomenon as it approaches Earth and the sun.
- Startup firm IG Drones, which was born out of the Veer Surendra Sai University of Technology (VSSUT) campus in Odisha's Sambalpur has developed a 5G-enabled drone that is capable of vertical take-off and landing. As it's a VTOL (Vertical Take-off and Landing), it can be operated from any terrain without the need for a conventional runway.
- Airtel-backed OneWeb successfully launched and deployed 40 satellites onboard a SpaceX launcher. This was the UK-based satellite network provider's 16th successful launch, bringing the total number of satellites in its low-Earth orbit (LEO) constellation of satellites up to 542. OneWeb originally sought to deploy a total of 648 satellites to enable its network of satellite-based internet connectivity around the world.
- The Centre is about to launch a five-year National Urban Technology Mission which is able to infuse technological improvements in municipal providers and infrastructure of 4,500 city native bodies within the nation. The mission, to be spearheaded by the ministry of housing and urban affairs, can have three main sub-heads. A be aware ready for the approval of the expenditure finance committee (EFC) pegs the mission outlay at ₹15,000 crore for 5 years.

- P. Sreekumar, the Satish Dhawan Professor at the Indian Space Research Organisation (ISRO) and advisor to its space science programme, stated that the organisation has not yet received approval from the Indian government for the Venus mission and that, as a result, the mission may be delayed until 2031. Shukrayaan I, the ISRO Venus mission, was scheduled to launch in December 2024.

- The entire country will be covered by Doppler Weather Radar Network by 2025 to help predict extreme weather events more accurately, union minister Jitendra Singh said, speaking at the foundation day of India Meteorological Department. Four new radars were added recently taking the number from 33 to 37. They include two at Murari Devi and Jot in Himachal Pradesh, and one each at Banihal Top in Jammu and Kashmir and Surkandaji in Uttarakhand covering a radius of 100 km.

- The National Aeronautics and Space Administration (NASA) announced that the James Webb Space Telescope has discovered its first new exoplanet. Researchers have labelled the planet as LHS 475 b, and it's roughly the same size as Earth. Located just 41 lightyears away, the planet orbits very close to a red dwarf star and completes a full orbit in just two days.

- MSN Group launched the 'world's first' generic Palbociclib tablets indicated for advanced breast cancer therapy under the brand Palborest. Palbociclib is approved by the USFDA, EMA and CDSCO in combination with hormonal therapies for patients with hormone receptor positive, human epidermal growth factor receptor negative locally advanced or metastatic breast cancer.

- Astronomers from McGill University in Canada and the Indian Institute of Science (IISc) in Bengaluru have used data from the Giant Metrewave Radio Telescope (GMRT) in Pune to detect a radio signal originating from atomic hydrogen in an extremely distant galaxy.

- NASA-JAXA Geotail spacecraft have signed off, after the failure of the spacecraft's remaining data recorder. Since its launch on July 24, 1992, Geotail orbited Earth, gathering an immense dataset on the structure and dynamics of the magnetosphere, Earth's protective magnetic bubble.

- Kerala reported 3 cases of norovirus, a gastro-intestinal zoonotic disease that is spread by intimate contact or contaminated food. The stomach flu and stomach bug are additional names for norovirus. But norovirus disease has nothing to do with the flu, which is brought on by an influenza virus. A SpaceX Falcon 9 rocket carried more than four dozen Starlink satellites into the low-Earth orbit in a launch from the California coast. The rocket lifted of at 7:43 a.m. California time from Vandenberg Space Force Base, located northwest of Santa Barbara. Fifty-one Starlink satellites were on board.

- Google AI Chatbot: Sundar Pichai, CEO of Google declared code red at Google in December to plan the development of Google's AI chatbot. According to the New York Times, Google has enlisted the assistance of two of its most well-known engineers, Larry Page and Sergey Brin, who no longer participate in day-to-day operations at the company.

- The United States space agency NASA has said the country plans to test a space-craft engine powered with nuclear fission by 2027, an advancement seen as key to long-haul missions including a manned journey to Mars. NASA will partner with the US military's Defense Advanced Research Projects Agency (DARPA) to develop the nuclear thermal propulsion engine and launch it into space, NASA administrator Bill Nelson said.

- Maria Valdes and three other scientists came upon a 17pound meteorite, which is heavier than the majority of bowling balls and pumpkins for Halloween, during an Antarctic mission in late December. The Field Museum in Chicago, where Valdes works, released a statement saying that only one out of every 450 or so meteorites discovered on the icy continent are this huge or greater.

- A team of scientists at Bengaluru's Jawaharlal Nehru Centre for Advanced Scientific Research (JNCASR), an autonomous institute of the Department of Science and Technology, Government of India, who were working on nitride-based materials has used their background for developing hardware for neuromorphic computing. They used ScN to develop a device mimicking a synapse that controls the signal transmission as well as remembers the signal.

- The first nasal vaccination produced in India against Covid-19, the iNCOVACC, was introduced by Science and Technology Minister Jitendra Singh and Union Health Minister Dr. Mansukh Mandaviya. Bharat Biotech has created the vaccine. At Mandaviya's house, the first intranasal vaccine produced in India was introduced to the world.

- The European Space Agency's Jupiter Icy Moons Explorer or JUICE is the next venture of humanity into the outer Solar System. It will be conducted thorough examinations of Jupiter, the largest planet in our solar system, and its three moons with oceans including Ganymede, Callisto, and Europa. The spacecraft has just completed its final tests before departing Toulouse, France, for Europe's Spaceport to count down to on April 2023 launch.

- Indian Institute of Astrophysics (IIA) handed over to ISR0, the Visible Line Emission Coronagraph (VELC), the primary payload on board Aditya-L1, which is India's first dedicated scientific mission to study the Sun, to be launched by June or July. The handing over ceremony was held in the presence of the ISR0 Chairman S Somanath at the Centre for Research and Education in Science and Technology (CREST) campus of IIA.

Books & Authors

- Former IAS officer Kaki Madhava Rao has authored a new book titled "Breaking Barriers: the Story of a Dalit Chief Secretary" which addresses the details about the dynamics of civil services at the ground level and also fills the gap in the knowledge about micro policies and governance.

- A Medical book 'Human Anatomy' in Hindi Manav sharir Rachna Vigyan was released by the Governor of Madhya Pradesh Shri Mangubhai Patel at the function which is a very useful book for the Medical students of all courses related to medical education written by Dr AK Dwivedi.

- Parliamentarian and author, Shashi Tharoor's latest book Ambedkar: A Life was recently launched at the Kitaab Kolkata event. In this new biography, Tharoor tells Ambedkar's story with great lucidity, insight, and admiration. He traces the arc of the great man's life from his birth into a family of Mahars in the Bombay Presidency on 14 April 1891 to his death in Delhi on 6 December 1956.

- Noted economist and popular historian Sanjeev Sanyal is set to release his latest book, "Revolutionaries: The Other Story of How India Won Its Freedom,".

- Former Chief Justice of India and member of the Rajya Sabha Ranjan Gogoi has released a book titled 'Chief Minister's Diary No.1' containing the account of events of the first year in office of Assam chief minister Himanta Biswa Sarma. The book featured accounts of daily activities he undertook as a chief minister.

- Journalist Tamal Bandyopadhyay has released his latest book "Roller Coaster: An Affair with Banking" with permission from Jaico Publishing House. Roller Coaster is a string of such stories and revelations from the country's foremost banking journalist's affair with the industry-even though banks were not ideal partners for such liaisons.

- Techno-educationalist, Professor K.K. Abdul Gaffar's autobiography, 'Njaan Sakshi' (me as the witness), was released by cricket legend Mahendra Singh Dhoni. The book was introduced by senior journalist T.A. Shafi. The first copy was received by Marwan Al Mulla, the CEO of Dubai Health Authority (DHA), from M S Dhoni. He also presented copies of the book to dignitaries including actor Tovino Thomas present at the occasion.

- Jadunama, a book written on veteran writer-lyricist Javed Akhtar by Arvind Mandloi, was released. Javed's wife, actor Shabana Azmi and children Zoya and Farhan Akhtar were present at the book launch. Farhan's wife, actor Shibani Dandekar also attended the event.

- Health and Family Welfare Minister Mansukh Mandaviya has officially launched the book titled "Braving A Viral Storm: India's Covid-19 Vaccine Story" in New Delhi. The book is co-authored by Aashish Chandorkar and Suraj Sudhir. The book launch comes ahead of India's second anniversary of starting its COVID-19 vaccination drive in January 2021.

- A new book "Irrfan Khan: A Life in Movies" will offer a compelling account of iconic actor Irrfan Khan's life and achievements, starting from his days at the prestigious National School of Drama (NSD) to his nearly a decadelong stint in television and his gradual ascent in the film industry. In the book, film critic Shubhra Gupta engages key people, including director Mira Nair, Vishal Bharadwaj, and Anurag Basu in conversation on the actor's art, craft and legacy.

- The English version of the book titled 'Come! Let's Run' by Tamil Nadu Health and Family Welfare Minister, Ma. Subramanian was released by Krishnamachari Srikkanth, former Captain of the Indian Cricket team. The Tamil version of the same book titled 'Odalam Vanga' was released on March 8, 2021. The book was published by Emerald Publishers and the English translation was done by Geeta Padmanaban (a teacher) along with J. Joicy and Sharon.

- A book titled 'COACHING BEYOND: My Days with the Indian Cricket Team' authored by R. Kaushik & R. Sridhar. The book reflects primarily on R. Sridhar's seven-year coaching tenure with the Indian cricket team as its fielding coach. This book isn't as technical as it is anecdotal. It throws light, for instance, on how Virat Kohli overcame a dismal Test series in England in 2014 to smash four hundreds in as many matches in his next overseas outing, in Australia.

- A book titled "India's Knowledge Supremacy: The New Dawn" Written by international Indian expat, Dr Ashwin Fernandes has released globally. This book was launched by Honourable Minister of Education of India Shri Dharmendra Pradhan, at an event at Dr Ambedkar International Centre. This New book launched focuses on India's knowledge supremacy, journey showcasing changing trends in newly emerging India.

Miscellaneous Current Affairs

- A team of astronomers led by scientists at the Indian Institute of Astrophysics and their international collaborators decided to study the most massive globular cluster system in our galaxy, Omega Centauri. They have detected strange hot stars in the cluster using the Ultraviolet Imaging Telescope (UVIT) image on AstroSat. They have found that these hot stars emitted much less ultraviolet radiation than expected from theoretical models and in comparison, with stars of another globular cluster, M13 has similar overall properties.

- India's first underwater metro service, The Kolkata Metro Rail Corporation (KMRC) said that the EastWest Metro Corridor project, is expected to be completed by December 2023. With this, another feather is being added to the crown of Kolkata Metro, the first metro railway in the country. Kolkata Metro, which started its journey in 1984, is being expanded to cover the whole city and its outskirts. The underwater metro, which will be running through the Hoogly river will connect the twin cities of Howrah and Kolkata.

- Union Home and Cooperation Minister Amit Shah inaugurated Mega Dairy at Mandya in Karnataka. The mega dairy inaugurated at a cost of Rs 260 crore would process 10 lakh liters of milk per day and will have the capacity to increase it upto

14 lakh liters per day. 10 lakh liters of milk is processed, prosperity reaches the homes of lakhs of farmers. There are 15,210 village level cooperative dairies in Karnataka, in which about 26.22 lakh farmers deliver their milk daily and through 16 district level dairies, Rs 28 crore is deposited into the accounts of 26 lakh farmers every day.

- 50 electric buses were launched in Delhi with support under the FAME India Phase II scheme of the Ministry of Heavy Industries. In 2019, the government approved Rs 10,000 crore for a period of three years. Out of total budgetary support, about 86 percent of the fund has been allocated for incentives so as to create demand for electric vehicles.
- Ghaziabad-Pt. Deen Dayal Upadhyay section (762 KM) becomes the longest fully automatic block signalling section of Indian Railways. In order to increase line capacity to run more trains on existing High-Density Routes of Indian Railways, Automatic Block Signalling (ABS) is a cost effective solution. Indian Railways has been rolling out Automatic Block signalling on a mission mode.
- The TRF came into existence in 2019 as a proxy outfit of the Lashkar-e-Taiba, a proscribed terrorist organisation. Home Ministry said that TRF is recruiting youth through online mediums for the furtherance of terrorist activities. Centre has declared The Resistance Front (TRF) as a terrorist organization under the Unlawful Activities (Prevention) Act, UAPA.
- The Ministry of Culture has informed the parliament that fifty of India's 3,693 centrally protected monuments have been missing. The submission of the missing report was done by the Ministry of Culture on 8th December 2022 to the Parliamentary Standing Committee on Transport, Tourism, and Culture as part of a report titled 'Issues relating to Untraceable Monuments and Protection of Monuments in India.' Many monuments and sites were lost to activities like urbanization, the construction of dams and reservoirs, and even encroachment. 14 Monuments have been lost due to rapid urbanization; 12 monuments are submerged by reservoirs while 24 are untraceable. There are total of 50 monuments missing.
- Union Minister for Fisheries, Animal Husbandry, and Dairying Parshottam Rupala inaugurated 29 Mobile Veterinary Units (MVU) and a Centralized call center in Thiruvananthapuram. It is a major step for benefit of the livestock farmers in Kerala.

- The International Kite Festival 2023 has began on 8 January in Ahmedabad, Gujarat. The festival, which is being organised after a gap of two years, was inaugurated by Chief Minister Bhupendra Patel. The previous edition was held in 2020 with 153 participants from 43 countries. The festival is being organised by Gujarat Tourism on the G20 theme of 'One Earth, One Family, One Future'. Apart from Ahmedabad, the International Kite Festival will also be organised in Surat, Vadodara, Rajkot, Dwarka, Somnath, Dhordo and Kevadia.

- Former India cricket team captain Mahendra Singh Dhoni and drone market Garuda Aerospace have launched a a surveillance drone named 'Droni.' Dhoni is an ambassador-cum-investor in the low-cost drone manufacturer. Dhoni had unveiled the camera drone called Droni at The Global Drone Expo in Chennai last year. Droni is a battery-operated quadcopter surveillance drone.

- A joint initiative by the Vidisha District Administration and the Centre for Development of Telematics (C-DOT), Department of Telecommunications (DoT), under the direction of Additional Secretary (Telecom) & Administrator USOF, made Vidisha, a district of Madhya Pradesh, the first district ever in India for on-ground implementation of groundbreaking 5G use cases proposed by startups.

- In an effort to test one's high-altitude endurance, a new challenge called "Soul of Steel" will be launched in India. Spearheaded by venture CLAW Global, which is run by veterans and supported by the Indian Army, the challenge will take place in the state of Uttarakhand and is similar to the "Ironman triathlon" long-distance triathlon challenge in Europe. The expedition will officially launch on January 14th, and will include 12 Indian participants and six international teams, with the age group for applicants being between 18 and 30 years.

- Union Minister of State for Culture Arjun Ram Meghwal handed over the 9th to 10th century Nataraja Idol of the Archeological Department official in Chittorgarh Fort in Rajasthan. Union Minister Arjun Ram Meghwal noted that there are only 13 idols of ancient importance that could be brought to India by the year 2023 but after 2014, Prime Minister Narendra Modi brought 229 idols to India.

- Regional carrier Flybig commenced its services from Itanagar to Guwahati. The Flybig carrier has commenced flights from Hollongi in Arunachal Pradesh to Guwahati in Assam. With this, Itanagar becomes the 10th destination on the Flybig network while the third destination in Arunachal Pradesh alone.

- A 63-year-old Italian man, Michele Santelia has achieved a world record by typing copies of 81 books backwards, a technique that he calls 'mirror writing', as per a report by the Guinness World Records (GWR). For the purpose of this record, the books must be typed using 'mirror writing', such that the result is the mirror image of any given language's normal writing.
- The Ministry of Environment, Forest and Climate Change (MoEF) has listed Neelakurinji under Schedule III of the Wildlife (Protection) Act, 1972, including it on the list of protected plants. Neelakurinji has been included in the list after the Center increased the earlier protected list of six plant species to 19. As per the order, those uprooting or destroying the plant will be fined Rs 25,000 and imprisoned for three years, furthermore, cultivation and possession of Neelakurinji are not permitted.
- The Archeological Survey of India (ASI) of the Patna circle has unearthed 1200 years old two miniature votive stupas near the Sarai Tila mound on the "Nalanda Mahavihara" grounds in the Nalanda district. The stupas found in Nalanda are carved from stones and depict Buddha figures. The Superintendent Archeologist, ASI Patna circle, Goutami Bhattacharya informed that at the beginning of the 7 th century CE, small miniature terracotta stupas became popular as votive offerings.
- Jammu and Kashmir's governments have declared the union territory as a "Free Area" for purposes of the Prevention and Control of Infectious and Contagious Diseases in Animals Act 2009. According to the notification issued by the government, the declaration has been made in the exercise of the power conferred by sub-section (5) of section 6 of the Prevention and Control of Infectious and Contagious Diseases in Animals (PCICDA) Act 2009.
- Jammu & Kashmir becomes the first union territory in India to completely switch to a digital method of administration, leading the way in the digital transformation of governance. All governmental and administrative services in Jammu & Kashmir are currently only offered digitally. - A Spanish great-grandmother who was born in the United States has likely become the world's oldest living person at 115, a Guinness World Records. The organisation shared that the woman named María Branyas Morera was born in March 1907 in the US and presently resides in Spain.
- Odisha State AIDS Control Society organised an awareness program on HIV AIDS in coordination with the Department of Sports and Youth Services and

Hockey India under the leadership of National AIDS Control Organization (NACO), on 19th January 2023.

- The Maharashtra Metro Rail Corporation (MahaMetro) has announced that the Commissioner of Metro Railway Safety (CMRS) will inspect a stretch of the Pune Metro in February, and clearances are expected in March. This line features India's deepest underground station, which will be ready in a few months at the Civil Court and measures 33.1 metres (108.59 feet) in depth.

- The Maharashtra Metro Rail Corporation (MahaMetro) has announced that the Commissioner of Metro Railway Safety (CMRS) will inspect a stretch of the Pune Metro in February, and clearances are expected in March. This line features India's deepest underground station, which will be ready in a few months at the Civil Court and measures 33.1 metres (108.59 feet) in depth.

- The American India Foundation (AIF) inaugurated India's first STEM Innovation and Learning Center (SILC) in the presence of the Minister for School Education, Thiru Anbil Mahesh Poyyamozhi. STEM Innovation and Learning Center is inaugurated under the scheme of Vanavil Mandram at the Government Higher Secondary School, MMDA Colony, Chennai.

- Lieutenant Governor R K Mathur launched the Unique Land Parcel Identification Number (ULPIN) in the Union Territory, with both hill councils of Kargil and Leh welcoming the initiative. The 14-digit ULPIN would help in the digitization of land records and also reach a conclusive land titling.

- The Jammu and Kashmir Government is set to host their first SARAS Fair 2023 from 4th February to 14th February 2023. In the SARAS Fair 2023, artisans and women's self-help groups from across the country will showcase their crafts, Handicrafts, handloom, and food. The fair would be organized at Bagh-e-Bahu, in Jammu.

- Union Territory Administrator, Banwari Lal Purohit has inaugurated northern India's largest floating solar power project of 2000kWp worth Rs 11.70 crore at waterworks, Sector 39, Chandigarh. The inauguration was held in the presence of MP Kirron Kher. He also inaugurated a 500kWp floating solar project with fountains at Dhanas Lake.

- East Coast Railways' Visakhapatnam railway station has received the prestigious 'Green Railway Station Certification' with the highest Platinum rating. The certificate has been awarded by the Indian Green Building Council (IGBC) for adopting green concepts. It secured 82 out of 100 points in six environmental categories.
- Google celebrates the 74th Republic Day of India with a creative masterpiece by a Gujarat-based guest artist Parth Kothekar. The Google Doodle finely illustrates the Republic Day Parade, along with some iconic landmarks like Rashtrapati Bhavan, the India Gate, the Daredevil motorcycle riders, and the CRFP marching contingent.
- The nation observes the 158th birth anniversary of the freedom fighter Lala Lajpat Rai, popularly known as Punjab Kesari. Lala Lajpat Rai was born on 28th January 1865 to his maternal grandparents in Dhudike. On the occasion of the 158th birth anniversary of the freedom fighter Lala Lajpat Rai, the cabinet minister announced a grant of Rs 12 lakh on the demand of the villagers.
- The month-long Khadi Fest- 23 was inaugurated by the Chairman of the Khadi and Village Industries Commission (KVIC) Mr. Manoj Kumar in Mumbai. In his inaugural address, Mr. Kumar said, events and exhibitions like Khadi Fest provide a platform to the Khadi Institutions, Prime Minister's Employment Generation Programme - PMEGP and Scheme of Fund for Regeneration of Traditional Industries - SFURTI units to market the products of thousands of artisans directly to customers.

Obituaries

- Statement released by the Vatican; the former Pope Benedict XVI has passed away in the Mater Ecclesiae Monastery in the Vatican. He was 95 years old. The head of the Catholic Church, former Pope Benedict, was the first pope in 600 years to resign.
- R Krishnakumar, a close confidante of Ratan Tata and a group veteran, passed away. Kerala-born Krishnakumar, who had served at multiple positions in the group, including heading its hospitality arm Indian Hotels, was 84. He had been active with the Tata Trusts after his retirement from executive roles and was reportedly a part of the team which worked alongside Ratan Tata in the Cyrus Mistry ouster episode. In 2009, Krishnakumar was awarded Padma Shri.

- Noted Rabindra Sangeet exponent, Sumitra Sen has passed away at the age of 89. She will be remembered for her rendition of songs like Jokhon Porbe Na Mor Sokhi Vabona Kahare Bole and Mone Ki Dwidha. Her rendition of Aaj Jyotsna Raate Shobai Gechhe Bone in Ritwik Ghatak's classic movie Komal Gandhar has remained a steadfast interpretation of the song. She was honoured with the Sangeet Mahasamman award by West Bengal government in 2012. - On October 11, 1968, three men boarded NASA's Saturn IB and had what the agency described as a "perfect launch" into space in the first crewed Apollo mission. On Tuesday, Walter Cunningham- the last surviving astronaut on that mission who helped pave the way for humans to walk on the moon - died in Houston. Walter was a fighter pilot, physicist and entrepreneur, above all, "he was an explorer."

- Gianluca Vialli, the former Italy and Chelsea striker, has died aged 58 after a long battle with pancreatic cancer. Gianluca Vialli was an Italian football player and manager who played as a striker. Vialli started his club career at Cremonese in 1980 in his native Italy where he made 105 league appearances scoring 23 goals. His performances impressed Sampdoria who signed him in 1984, and with whom he scored 85 league goals, won three Italian cups, Serie A and the European Cup Winners Cup.

- Senior leader of the Bharatiya Janata Party (BJP) and former West Bengal governor, Keshari Nath Tripathi passed away at 88. Born on November 10, 1934 in erstwhile Allahabad, Tripathi was also a senior advocate at the Allahabad High Court. He joined RSS when he was just 12 and later switched to Bharatiya Jana Sangh. He was jailed in Naini Central Jail in 1953 for participating in the 'Kashmir Andolan' and again in 1990 for taking part in the Ram Janmabhoomi movement.

- Padma Awardee Dr Tehemton Erach Udwadia, an Indian Surgeon and Gastroenterologist, who was known as the 'father of laparoscopic surgery in India' passed away, at the age of 88. He was born on 15th July 1934 in the Bombay Presidency, British India (now Mumbai, Maharashtra, India).

- Socialist stalwart and former JD(U) chief Sharad Yadav passed away. He was 75 . He is survived by his wife, daughter and son. A 7-term Lok Sabha and 4-term Rajya Sabha member, Yadav, a former Union Minister, had not been keeping well for some time.

- A british linguist and educator specialised in Dravidian languages, Ronald E. Asher has passed away at the age of 96. A fellow of the Royal Asiatic Society, London, Asher won a gold medal from Kerala Sahitya Akademi, Trichur, in 1983 and was honoured by the Royal Society, Edinburgh in 1991. He was also a recipient of a medal from College de France, Paris in 1970.

- Ray Cordeiro, who interviewed music acts including the Beatles during a six-decade career on Hong Kong radio that earned him the title of the world's longest-working disc jockey, has passed away. Cordeiro, who was born in Hong Kong in 1924 of Portuguese descent, was recognized by the Guinness Book of Records as the world's longest-working DJ. - The last Nizam of Hyderabad, Mukarram Jah Bahadur, who passed away night in Turkey, will be buried in the family vault in the Mecca Masjid courtyard. The preparation of the vault where other members of the Nizam's family who governed Hyderabad starting in 1724 are buried was overseen by representatives of the Nizam Trust.

- Italian film legend Gina Lollobrigida, the diva who came to represent Italy's vibrant rebirth after World War Two during the 1950s has passed away at the age of 95.

- AD Damodaran, leading scientist and former director of the CSIR-National Institute for Interdisciplinary Science and Technology (NIIST), passed away in Thiruvananthapuram at the age of 87 . He also served as the Chairman of the Kerala State Council for Science, Technology and Environment.

- The world's oldest person, French nun Lucile Randon, has died aged 118. Randon, also known as Sister Andre, was born in southern France on February 11, 1904, a decade before World War I. She was long regarded as the oldest European, but the death of Japan's Kane Tanaka at the age of 119 last year made her the world's oldest person.

- Padma Shri Awardee Prabhaben Sobhagchand Shah passed away on 18th January 2023 at the age of 92 . Prabhaben Sobhagchand Shah was a social worker from the Union Territory of Dadra and Nagar Haveli, Daman, and Diu. Prabhaben Sobhagchand Shah was also known as "Daman ki Divya".

- David Crosby, the father of American folk-rock, has passed away at the age of 81. He was influential musical pioneer of the 1960s and 1970s who created a distinctly

American brand of folk-rock with the Byrds and later with Crosby, Stills, Nash and Young.

- Renowned Assamese poet and recipient of Jnapith Award, Nilamani Phookan has passed away. He was 89. Phookan was one of the most celebrated poet of Assam and has been awarded the country's highest literary award, the 56th Jnanpith for the year 2021. The notable works of Phukan are 'Xurjya Henu Naami Aahe Ei Nodiyedi', 'Kabita', and 'Gulapi Jamur Lagna'.

- Former Vice Chief of Air Staff Air Marshal Harjeet Singh Arora passed away at the age of 61. Air Marshal Harjit Singh Arora PVSM, AVSM, ADC (25 June 1961 - 21 January 2023) was an officer of the Indian Air Force and served as the Vice Chief of the Air Staff from 1 October 2019 to 30 June 2021.

- Dr Balkrishna Vithaldas Doshi, who is widely revered for his contribution in the field of architecture, has passed away. He was 95. For his outstanding contribution to the field of architecture, he was conferred with Pritzker Prize in 2018 and the coveted Padma Shri in 1976. The Royal Institute of British Architects (RIBA) has announced that Indian architect Balkrishna Doshi will be the recipient of the 2022 Royal Gold Medal.

- 'Ironman of India' Sabir Ali, who won the decathlon gold at the 1981 Asian Athletics Championships in Tokyo, passed away. He was 67. Ali, who retired from Railways, won the title in the Japanese capital with a tally of 7,253 points beating Japan's Nobuya Saito (7,078) and China's Zu Qilin (7,074). He also won two silver medals at the South Asian Federation Games held in Kathmandu and Dhaka.

- Veteran Telugu film actor and former parliamentarian J Jamuna passed away at the age of 86. She was born in Hampi on August 30, 1936, Jamuna made her film debut at the age of 16 with Puttillu (1952) made by Garikapati Raja Rao of Praja Natya Mandali, cultural wing of the Communist Party of India (CPI). Before that she acted in several stage plays on behalf of Indian People's Theatre Association floated by Raja Rao.

www.ingramcontent.com/pod-product-compliance
Ingram Content Group UK Ltd.
Pitfield, Milton Keynes, MK11 3LW, UK
UKHW061704190726
13853UKWH00008B/2399

9 789355 566515